Reading Comprehension
Test Taking Skills
Grade 3

Best Value Books™

by
Patricia Pedigo
and
Dr. Roger DeSanti

ISBN 0-88724-476-9

Table of Contents

About the book

This book is just one in our Best Value™ series of reproducible, skill-oriented activity books. Standardized tests have become a typical means of student achievement evaluation. Many students may not perform as well as they might on these tests simply due to a lack of practice in test taking and/or a lack of understanding of the task presented. This book is designed to provide practice activities for appropriate application of reading comprehension and test taking strategies.

The passages presented in this book cover a variety of word skills and real reading situations including narrative, expository, directions, and letters. The passage questions are presented in a typical standardized testing format that targets specific levels of comprehension (literal, inferential, applied, and prediction or judgmental). Each level of comprehension calls for different strategies that are discussed in detail on the pages titled "Levels of Comprehension." It is the authors' contention that children should be made aware of these levels of comprehension and the associated strategies for each. Providing the children with these comprehension tools gives them an organized approach to answering questions about any given passage.

Also included in this book is a list of Test Taking Tips for students, found on page vi. This list includes many strategies that may be helpful in a variety of test taking situations (true and false, multiple choice, and matching).

About the authors

Patricia Pedigo has many years of teaching experience in urban, rural, public, and private settings. She has taught all elementary and middle school grade levels and has been a reading specialist. While teaching at the University of New Orleans, Patricia professed her belief in finding creative ways to teach through practical applications. She has created many materials that incorporate a reading approach integrating content areas and language development. She holds an M.Ed. in Reading Education.

Dr. Roger DeSanti has been an educator since the mid 1970's. His teaching experiences have spanned a wide range of grade and ability levels from deaf nursery through university graduate school. As a professor, he has authored numerous articles and books, achievement tests, and instructional materials.

Levels of Comprehension

There are many levels at which we may comprehend text, ranging from very simple to deeply complex. There are several different models of comprehension that demonstrate these levels in a detailed manner. However, we found that a simple version of these models is most effective with children. Below is a short passage followed by a discussion of four levels of comprehension, example questions, and strategies to employ when answering the questions.

> Ben sat on the front steps. His chin was cupped in his hand and tears were trickling down his cheeks. On the step beside Ben lay a leash with the name "Rags" embossed on the leather. Ben had looked everywhere he could think, but it was no use.

Literal

Literal comprehension is an understanding of what has been clearly stated in the passage. Questions that require literal comprehension will ask for information that has been given. For example:

1. What is the name of the boy in this story? (Ben)
2. Where is Ben sitting? (on the front steps)
3. What is on the step next to Ben? (a leash)

The best strategy for answering literal comprehension questions is simply to look back at the text and find the answer.

Inferential

Inferential comprehension is the ability to understand the implied message of the text. Questions that require inferential comprehension will ask for information that is suggested but never directly stated in the text. For example:

1. How is Ben feeling? (sad)

To answer an inferential comprehension question the reader needs to find clues that imply the meaning. For the example question, it is necessary to look at the stated information that gives a hint as to how Ben may be feeling. The example states that Ben's "chin was cupped in his hand," a behavior that usually accompanies boredom or sadness. The second clue given is that "tears were trickling down his cheeks." These two pieces of information imply that Ben is sad.

Levels of Comprehension

> Ben sat on the front steps. His chin was cupped in his hand and tears were trickling down his cheeks. On the step beside Ben lay a leash with the name "Rags" embossed on the leather. Ben had looked every-where he could think, but it was no use.

Applied

Applied comprehension requires that the reader use the stated and implied information and apply it to what he/she already knows about such situations. This level of comprehension takes the reader beyond the text and into his/her own knowledge base. For example:

1. Who is Rags? (a dog, cat, or other pet)
2. Why do you think Ben is sad? (He cannot find Rags.)

To answer an applied comprehension question the reader must extract the stated and implied information, compare and contrast it to his/her general knowledge, and arrive at a logical conclusion. To answer question number one, it is necessary to understand that: the name "Rags" is embossed on the leash (stated information); Ben cares about Rags (implied information); and that leashes are used for walking pets (general knowledge). To answer question number two, it is necessary to understand that: Ben had been looking for something (stated information); he could not find what he was looking for (implied information); Rags is probably what is missing (implied); and lost pets often make children sad (general knowledge).

Judgmental

Judgmental comprehension is the level at which the reader can process the information to arrive at an opinion or prediction that can be justified or supported with facts. For example:

1. What else might Ben do to find Rags?

To answer a judgmental comprehension question the reader must form an opinion or prediction that is logical to the story. There may be many acceptable answers, but they must be supported by the facts from the story and/or real life situations. For example, a child may answer, "I would put up posters of Rags with my phone number. That is what my friend did when she lost her dog. Ben wants to find Rags and the neighbors might be able to help."

Test Taking Tips

True and False

- Read the question carefully. If any part is false, mark the answer false.
- Look for key words like the words listed below. Think about what the words mean.

always	only	never	all
usually	every	frequently	often

Multiple Choice

- Read the question carefully. See if you know the answer <u>before</u> you look at the choices.
- Read <u>all</u> the choices, even if the first choice seems right.
- If you don't know which answer is correct, cross out the answers you know are <u>wrong</u>. Then, pick from the choices that are left.
- Always put down an answer. If you leave it blank, you know it is wrong. A guess might be right!

Matching

- Match the answers you know first.
- When you've made a match, cross out the number so you know it has been used.
- If you aren't sure, guess!

Ready-To-Use Ideas and Activities

The activities in this book will help children master the basic skills necessary to become competent test takers. Remember, as you read through the activities listed below, and as you go through this book, that all children learn at their own rate. Although repetition is important, it is critical that we never lose sight of the fact that it is equally important to build children's self-esteem and self-confidence if we want them to become successful learners.

Practice Test Taking

Reproduce the pages in this book to administer as a test to the students. Answers should be marked by completely darkening the "bubble" next to the selected choice. Practice tests may be administered in various ways: You may wish to select one practice sheet from each skill and give each student a "packet" similar to the standardized testing procedure. When the students are familiar with the practice test format, give them a practice timed test as most standardized tests are timed. It is suggested that three to five minutes be given for each page and that no test packet should exceed twenty minutes. You may also use the book as practice to reinforce particular skills.

Flash Cards

The back of this book has removable flash cards that will be great for use in basic skill and enrichment activities. Pull the flash cards out and cut them apart. If you have access to a paper cutter, use it to cut the flash cards apart. The following is just one of the ways you may want to use these flash cards.

Reproduce the bingo sheet on the next page in this book, making enough copies to have one for each student. Hand them out to the students. Take the flash cards and write the words on the chalk board. Have the students choose 24 of the words and write them in any order on the empty spaces of their bingo cards, writing only one word in each space. When all students have finished their cards, take the flash cards and make them into a deck. Call out the words one at a time. Any student who has a word that is called out should make an "X" through the word to cross it out. The first student who crosses out five words in a row (horizontally, vertically, or diagonally) wins the game. To extend the game, continue playing until a student crosses out all the words on his bingo sheet.

Vocabulary Bingo

		FREE		

Name _____

DIRECTIONS:
One or more letters are underlined in each of the words below. Read each word, then mark the space for the word that has the same sound as the underlined letter or letters.

1. <u>a</u>nswer

plant	late	lazy
○	○	○

2. stu<u>d</u>y

ribbon	blame	different
○	○	○

3. photo<u>gr</u>aph

grace	gurgle	scarf
○	○	○

4. stea<u>m</u>

insect	muscle	teen
○	○	○

5. f<u>or</u>ce

ordinary	robin	wrote
○	○	○

6. over<u>s</u>leep

slant	salt	clean
○	○	○

7. No<u>v</u>ember

fault	punish	veil
○	○	○

8. <u>bl</u>ame

bullet	problem	ball
○	○	○

9. happ<u>e</u>n

meet	zebra	often
○	○	○

10. p<u>i</u>lot

icy	begin	silver
○	○	○

11. tomorr<u>ow</u>

somehow	crown	groan
○	○	○

12. e<u>qu</u>ipment

punish	quarter	kingdom
○	○	○

13. <u>th</u>umb

what	both	trace
○	○	○

14. appl<u>y</u>

hind	uneasy	noisy
○	○	○

Name _____

DIRECTIONS:
One or more letters are underlined in each of the words below. Read each word, then mark the space for the word that has the same sound as the underlined letter or letters.

1. anoth<u>er</u>		
operate ○	each ○	ears ○
2. ob<u>j</u>ect		
goal ○	giant ○	grab ○
3. cr<u>a</u>zy		
about ○	mail ○	hand ○
4. chil<u>dr</u>en		
dirt ○	chart ○	dream ○
5. cou<u>gh</u>		
famous ○	ghastly ○	daughter ○
6. <u>n</u>oisy		
harm ○	handle ○	moist ○
7. underst<u>oo</u>d		
balloon ○	crook ○	shampoo ○

8. tomat<u>o</u>		
unfold ○	perform ○	proof ○
9. ch<u>oi</u>ce		
echo ○	canoe ○	enjoy ○
10. li<u>br</u>ary		
bird ○	broken ○	rib ○
11. befor<u>e</u>		
sweet ○	better ○	care ○
12. descr<u>i</u>be		
isn't ○	until ○	quiet ○
13. pl<u>ow</u>		
powder ○	own ○	blow ○
14. f<u>i</u>replace		
rare ○	sneeze ○	swell ○

Name _____

DIRECTIONS:
One or more letters are underlined in each of the words below. Read each word, then mark the space for the word that has the same sound as the underlined letter or letters.

1. sma<u>sh</u>				8. weal<u>th</u>		
sample ○	blacksmith ○	shame ○		thirty ○	shelf ○	hoot ○
2. for<u>w</u>ard				9. free<u>z</u>e		
reply ○	velvet ○	waist ○		mushroom ○	moccasin ○	easy ○
3. bou<u>gh</u>t				10. str<u>ea</u>k		
hire ○	bright ○	gather ○		parent ○	prize ○	remain ○
4. <u>bl</u>eed				11. t<u>oo</u>		
tumbler ○	label ○	bald ○		toot ○	so ○	wool ○
5. b<u>ou</u>nce				12. h<u>ur</u>tle		
drove ○	should ○	count ○		Thursday ○	park ○	rust ○
6. su<u>gg</u>est				13. ch<u>ar</u>ge		
jail ○	giggle ○	gentle ○		trade ○	hear ○	army ○
7. <u>a</u>gain				14. <u>c</u>ent		
ahead ○	day ○	lady ○		crest ○	since ○	cart ○

Name _____

DIRECTIONS:
One or more letters are underlined in each of the words below. Read each word, then mark the space for the word that has the same sound as the underlined letter or letters.

1. be<u>c</u>ome

circus	king	cell
○	○	○

8. d<u>e</u>ntist

greed	deal	fetch
○	○	○

2. aw<u>f</u>ul

photo	clear	punish
○	○	○

9. del<u>i</u>ght

ghost	false	sigh
○	○	○

3. thi<u>r</u>teen

riddle	timid	circus
○	○	○

10. lu<u>ng</u>

naughty	length	grand
○	○	○

4. r<u>oy</u>al

moist	aloud	money
○	○	○

11. kangar<u>oo</u>

flute	furry	bookcase
○	○	○

5. purpo<u>s</u>e

please	walrus	crazy
○	○	○

12. <u>sn</u>uggle

snatch	sunflower	singer
○	○	○

6. dis<u>tr</u>ust

turkey	tore	traffic
○	○	○

13. a<u>wh</u>ile

wrench	saw	wheat
○	○	○

7. h<u>a</u>zy

above	April	animal
○	○	○

14. <u>o</u>dd

golden	open	mop
○	○	○

Name _____

Skill: Word Study—Test 5

DIRECTIONS:
One or more letters are underlined in each of the words below. Read each word, then mark the space for the word that has the same sound as the underlined letter or letters.

1. t<u>ow</u>er			8. sh<u>oo</u>k		
tow ○	snow ○	hour ○	igloo ○	afoot ○	broom ○

2. thr<u>ow</u>n			9. l<u>oo</u>p		
comfort ○	famous ○	dinosaur ○	cookie ○	tooth ○	football ○

3. th<u>ou</u>sand			10. <u>a</u>ll		
tough ○	though ○	ourselves ○	above ○	yawn ○	fast ○

4. f<u>e</u>male			11. <u>fl</u>avor		
empty ○	equal ○	ever ○	firm ○	film ○	afloat ○

5. be<u>h</u>ave			12. ob<u>j</u>ect		
photo ○	hamburger ○	furniture ○	danger ○	glue ○	grain ○

6. f<u>o</u>llow			13. sec<u>o</u>nd		
November ○	okay ○	olive ○	photo ○	mother ○	explode ○

7. hea<u>p</u>			14. pre<u>s</u>ent		
punish ○	graph ○	afraid ○	juice ○	frost ○	musical ○

Name _____

DIRECTIONS:
One or more letters are underlined in each of the words below. Read each word, then mark the space for the word that has the same sound as the underlined letter or letters.

1. insp<u>e</u>ct

separate	sip	spook
○	○	○

8. be<u>tw</u>een

twinkle	tower	thrown
○	○	○

2. <u>wr</u>inkle

wore	worn	rewrite
○	○	○

9. comm<u>a</u>

space	away	label
○	○	○

3. sp<u>are</u>

jaw	cause	careful
○	○	○

10. pit<u>ch</u>er

charm	cream	cast
○	○	○

4. degr<u>ee</u>

deaf	least	meadow
○	○	○

11. a<u>fr</u>aid

friend	refuse	farewell
○	○	○

5. sl<u>i</u>t

fry	inch	jail
○	○	○

12. mar<u>k</u>et

fancy	face	picture
○	○	○

6. <u>o</u>vernight

hopeful	pilot	odd
○	○	○

13. <u>j</u>oin

crow	newsboy	hour
○	○	○

7. <u>a</u>lphabet

great	pooh	careful
○	○	○

14. de<u>scr</u>ibe

secret	slice	scout
○	○	○

Name _____

DIRECTIONS:
One or more letters are underlined in each of the words below. Read each word, then mark the space for the word that has the same sound as the underlined letter or letters.

1. thir<u>st</u>

visitor	pleasant	pasture
○	○	○

8. <u>u</u>nfold

flute	munch	gurgle
○	○	○

2. rela<u>x</u>

skin	mixture	square
○	○	○

9. c<u>au</u>se

caught	although	blow
○	○	○

3. c<u>ar</u>d

March	author	bare
○	○	○

10. <u>c</u>limb

coal	call	click
○	○	○

4. p<u>ea</u>ch

ahead	feather	week
○	○	○

11. wi<u>gg</u>le

neighbor	gentle	gang
○	○	○

5. t<u>i</u>de

mill	slice	laid
○	○	○

12. <u>kn</u>elt

keeper	kettle	unlike
○	○	○

6. zer<u>o</u>

obey	onion	nor
○	○	○

13. c<u>ou</u>nt

outside	noble	object
○	○	○

7. <u>p</u>lastic

flop	explore	flipper
○	○	○

14. sun<u>sh</u>ine

shelf	school	scrap
○	○	○

Name _____

DIRECTIONS:
One or more letters are underlined in each of the words below. Read each word, then mark the space for the word that has the same sound as the underlined letter or letters.

1. sweater

tower	swoop	twist
○	○	○

8. future

umbrella	January	sudden
○	○	○

2. yawn

beyond	scurry	heavy
○	○	○

9. drift

excite	attic	ice cream
○	○	○

3. number

grab	color	did
○	○	○

10. bread

meat	beat	ahead
○	○	○

4. secret

race	crayon	carol
○	○	○

11. glitter

hourglass	lung	dull
○	○	○

5. croak

motor	ribbon	gown
○	○	○

12. coffee

broil	round	along
○	○	○

6. surprise

reply	present	perch
○	○	○

13. skeleton

snack	peck	basketball
○	○	○

7. report

tomorrow	gather	thank
○	○	○

14. bushy

figure	duty	pudding
○	○	○

Name _____

DIRECTIONS:
One or more letters are underlined in each of the words below. Read each word, then mark the space for the word that has the same sound as the underlined letter or letters.

1. bel**ly**

myself ○   depend ○   money ○

8. kn**i**fe

drip ○   continue ○   hire ○

2. t**y**pe

grand ○   maid ○   lighthouse ○

9. villag**e**r

graham ○   fingertip ○   range ○

3. warm**th**

tongue ○   tank ○   thick ○

10. **g**rin

gruff ○   guard ○   girl ○

4. **fl**ame

half ○   floppy ○   perform ○

11. mi**st**

sixth ○   scarf ○   stamp ○

5. chu**ck**le

collection ○   center ○   side ○

12. fran**k**

squirrel ○   coach ○   dune ○

6. **a**che

fancy ○   escape ○   farewell ○

13. ai**m**

famous ○   chair ○   nickel ○

7. dist**ur**b

turn ○   rust ○   rub ○

14. f**au**lt

owe ○   water ○   sauce ○

Name _____

DIRECTIONS:
In each question the same word is divided into syllables in three different ways. Decide which is the correct way to divide the word and mark the answer.

1. ○ a•board
   ○ ab•oard
   ○ abo•ard

2. ○ a•ccount
   ○ ac•count
   ○ accou•nt

3. ○ bi•rdhouse
   ○ bird•house
   ○ birdho•use

4. ○ de•pend
   ○ dep•end
   ○ depe•nd

5. ○ ba•ckward
   ○ back•ward
   ○ backw•ard

6. ○ chi•pmunk
   ○ chipm•unk
   ○ chip•munk

7. ○ e•yelash
   ○ eye•lash
   ○ eyel•ash

8. ○ mi•llion
   ○ mil•lion
   ○ milli•on

9. ○ h•obby
   ○ ho•bby
   ○ hob•by

10. ○ mo•ment
    ○ mom•ent
    ○ mome•nt

11. ○ mu•mble
    ○ mum•ble
    ○ mumb•le

12. ○ li•mit
    ○ lim•it
    ○ limi•t

13. ○ n•arrow
    ○ na•rrow
    ○ nar•row

14. ○ foo•tprint
    ○ foot•print
    ○ footpr•int

15. ○ spid•er
    ○ sp•ider
    ○ spi•der

16. ○ pl•anet
    ○ pla•net
    ○ plan•et

17. ○ pro•gram
    ○ prog•ram
    ○ progr•am

18. ○ stu•bborn
    ○ stub•born
    ○ stubb•orn

Name _____

DIRECTIONS:
In each question the same word is divided into syllables in three different ways. Decide which is the correct way to divide the word and mark the answer.

1. ○ re•peat
   ○ rep•eat
   ○ repe•at

2. ○ re•ply
   ○ rep•ly
   ○ repl•y

3. ○ fl•utter
   ○ flu•tter
   ○ flut•ter

4. ○ r•eward
   ○ re•ward
   ○ rew•ard

5. ○ st•ation
   ○ sta•tion
   ○ stat•ion

6. ○ se•aweed
   ○ seaw•eed
   ○ sea•weed

7. ○ swim•mer
   ○ sw•immer
   ○ swimm•er

8. ○ pr•epare
   ○ pre•pare
   ○ prep•are

9. ○ tre•etop
   ○ tree•top
   ○ treet•op

10. ○ a•corn
    ○ ac•orn
    ○ aco•rn

11. ○ be•rry
    ○ ber•ry
    ○ berr•y

12. ○ bugg•y
    ○ bu•ggy
    ○ bug•gy

13. ○ bla•ckboard
    ○ black•board
    ○ blackb•oard

14. ○ co•mplain
    ○ comp•lain
    ○ com•plain

15. ○ e•xpert
    ○ ex•pert
    ○ exp•ert

16. ○ blu•ebird
    ○ blueb•ird
    ○ blue•bird

17. ○ gold•fish
    ○ gol•dfish
    ○ goldf•ish

18. ○ ho•llow
    ○ holl•ow
    ○ hol•low

Name _____

DIRECTIONS:
In each question the same word is divided into syllables in three different ways. Decide which is the correct way to divide the word and mark the answer.

1. ○ froz•en
    ○ fro•zen
    ○ fr•ozen

2. ○ m•aple
    ○ ma•ple
    ○ map•le

3. ○ fli•pper
    ○ flip•per
    ○ flipp•er

4. ○ m•edal
    ○ me•dal
    ○ med•al

5. ○ men•tion
    ○ ment•ion
    ○ me•ntion

6. ○ pa•ckage
    ○ pac•kage
    ○ pack•age

7. ○ ta•lent
    ○ tal•ent
    ○ tale•nt

8. ○ pri•vate
    ○ priv•ate
    ○ priva•te

9. ○ pa•rent
    ○ par•ent
    ○ pare•nt

10. ○ st•udent
    ○ stu•dent
    ○ stud•ent

11. ○ pa•ttern
    ○ pat•tern
    ○ patt•ern

12. ○ pu•nish
    ○ pun•ish
    ○ puni•sh

13. ○ he•lmet
    ○ hel•met
    ○ helm•et

14. ○ po•lite
    ○ pol•ite
    ○ poli•te

15. ○ per•form
    ○ perf•orm
    ○ perfo•rm

16. ○ s•olid
    ○ so•lid
    ○ sol•id

17. ○ ro•wboat
    ○ row•boat
    ○ rowbo•at

18. ○ re•ceive
    ○ rec•eive
    ○ rece•ive

Name _____

DIRECTIONS:
In each question the same word is divided into syllables in three different ways. Decide which is the correct way to divide the word and mark the answer.

1. ○ tr•umpet
   ○ trum•pet
   ○ trump•et

2. ○ a•ddress
   ○ ad•dress
   ○ add•ress

3. ○ bu•cket
   ○ buc•ket
   ○ buck•et

4. ○ a•wful
   ○ aw•ful
   ○ awf•ul

5. ○ com•mand
   ○ co•mmand
   ○ comm•and

6. ○ de•tail
   ○ det•ail
   ○ deta•il

7. ○ cu•rtain
   ○ cur•tain
   ○ curt•ain

8. ○ cac•tus
   ○ ca•ctus
   ○ cact•us

9. ○ in•sect
   ○ ins•ect
   ○ inse•ct

10. ○ fre•edom
    ○ freed•om
    ○ free•dom

11. ○ o•bject
    ○ ob•ject
    ○ obj•ect

12. ○ harv•est
    ○ har•vest
    ○ harve•st

13. ○ le•vel
    ○ lev•el
    ○ leve•l

14. ○ out•line
    ○ outl•ine
    ○ ou•tline

15. ○ gr•umpy
    ○ grum•py
    ○ grump•y

16. ○ nec•klace
    ○ neck•lace
    ○ neckl•ace

17. ○ pa•lace
    ○ pal•ace
    ○ pala•ce

18. ○ sh•aggy
    ○ sha•ggy
    ○ shag•gy

Name _____

DIRECTIONS:
In each question the same word is divided into syllables in three different ways. Decide which is the correct way to divide the word and mark the answer.

1. ○ re•main
   ○ rem•ain
   ○ rema•in

2. ○ pa•rtner
   ○ par•tner
   ○ part•ner

3. ○ rep•lace
   ○ repl•ace
   ○ re•place

4. ○ st•upid
   ○ stu•pid
   ○ stup•id

5. ○ gra•ceful
   ○ gracef•ul
   ○ grace•ful

6. ○ su•pply
   ○ supp•ly
   ○ sup•ply

7. ○ rail•road
   ○ railro•ad
   ○ rai•lroad

8. ○ po•wder
   ○ pow•der
   ○ powd•er

9. ○ pi•lot
   ○ p•ilot
   ○ pil•ot

10. ○ se•ttle
    ○ set•tle
    ○ sett•le

11. ○ t•ulip
    ○ tu•lip
    ○ tul•ip

12. ○ air•port
    ○ airp•ort
    ○ ai•rport

13. ○ co•llar
    ○ coll•ar
    ○ col•lar

14. ○ bi•scuit
    ○ bisc•uit
    ○ bis•cuit

15. ○ bu•ndle
    ○ bun•dle
    ○ bund•le

16. ○ excu•se
    ○ ex•cuse
    ○ e•xcuse

17. ○ con•fuse
    ○ co•nfuse
    ○ conf•use

18. ○ a•nger
    ○ an•ger
    ○ ang•er

Name _____

DIRECTIONS:
In each question the same word is divided into syllables in three different ways. Decide which is the correct way to divide the word and mark the answer.

1. ○ mi•stake
   ○ mis•take
   ○ mist•ake

2. ○ hom•eade
   ○ homea•de
   ○ home•ade

3. ○ ma•nger
   ○ man•ger
   ○ mang•er

4. ○ mu•ddy
   ○ mud•dy
   ○ mudd•y

5. ○ hu•man
   ○ hum•an
   ○ h•uman

6. ○ gi•ggle
   ○ gig•gle
   ○ gigg•le

7. ○ kin•gdom
   ○ king•dom
   ○ kingd•om

8. ○ i•mprove
   ○ imp•rove
   ○ im•prove

9. ○ pri•ncess
   ○ prin•cess
   ○ princ•ess

10. ○ ta•ngle
    ○ tang•le
    ○ tan•gle

11. ○ pro•tect
    ○ prot•ect
    ○ pr•otect

12. ○ scatt•er
    ○ sca•tter
    ○ scat•ter

13. ○ she•pherd
    ○ shep•herd
    ○ sheph•erd

14. ○ su•ccess
    ○ suc•cess
    ○ succ•ess

15. ○ re•scue
    ○ res•cue
    ○ resc•ue

16. ○ surf•ace
    ○ su•rface
    ○ sur•face

17. ○ se•ason
    ○ sea•son
    ○ seas•on

18. ○ ro•bin
    ○ rob•in
    ○ r•obin

Name _____

DIRECTIONS:
In each question the same word is divided into syllables in three different ways. Decide which is the correct way to divide the word and mark the answer.

1. ○ six•teen
   ○ sixt•een
   ○ sixte•en

2. ○ sy•mbol
   ○ sym•bol
   ○ symb•ol

3. ○ twent•y
   ○ twe•nty
   ○ twen•ty

4. ○ a•larm
   ○ al•arm
   ○ ala•rm

5. ○ de•mand
   ○ dem•and
   ○ dema•nd

6. ○ co•mfort
   ○ com•fort
   ○ comf•ort

7. ○ che•erful
   ○ chee•rful
   ○ cheer•ful

8. ○ ba•ker
   ○ bak•er
   ○ bake•r

9. ○ e•ager
   ○ ea•ger
   ○ eag•er

10. ○ bar•nyard
    ○ barn•yard
    ○ barny•ard

11. ○ hai•rcut
    ○ hair•cut
    ○ haric•ut

12. ○ la•undry
    ○ lau•ndry
    ○ laun•dry

13. ○ ho•oray
    ○ hoo•ray
    ○ hoor•ay

14. ○ flas•hlight
    ○ flash•light
    ○ flashl•ight

15. ○ hu•nger
    ○ hun•ger
    ○ hung•er

16. ○ li•quid
    ○ liq•uid
    ○ liqu•id

17. ○ na•ture
    ○ nat•ure
    ○ natur•e

18. ○ pr•event
    ○ pre•vent
    ○ prev•ent

Name _____

DIRECTIONS:
In each question the same word is divided into syllables in three different ways. Decide which is the correct way to divide the word and mark the answer.

1. ○ sa•ddle
   ○ sad•dle
   ○ sadd•le

2. ○ safe•ty
   ○ saf•ety
   ○ sa•fety

3. ○ spr•inkle
   ○ sprin•kle
   ○ sprink•le

4. ○ te•mper
   ○ temp•er
   ○ tem•per

5. ○ school•work
   ○ scho•olwork
   ○ schoolw•ork

6. ○ sho•elace
   ○ shoel•ace
   ○ shoe•lace

7. ○ stai•rway
   ○ sta•irway
   ○ stair•way

8. ○ sur•round
   ○ surr•ound
   ○ su•rround

9. ○ pe•tal
   ○ pet•al
   ○ peta•l

10. ○ som•eplace
    ○ some•place
    ○ somepl•ace

11. ○ ru•bber
    ○ rub•ber
    ○ rubb•er

12. ○ tra•ffic
    ○ traf•fic
    ○ traff•ic

13. ○ u•nfair
    ○ un•fair
    ○ unf•air

14. ○ un•wrap
    ○ unw•rap
    ○ unwr•ap

15. ○ wi•ggle
    ○ wig•gle
    ○ wigg•le

16. ○ camp•fire
    ○ cam•pfire
    ○ campfi•re

17. ○ ben•eath
    ○ bene•ath
    ○ be•neath

18. ○ day•dream
    ○ daydr•eam
    ○ daydre•am

Name _____

DIRECTIONS:
In each question the same word is divided into syllables in three different ways. Decide which is the correct way to divide the word and mark the answer.

1. ○ car•dboard
   ○ card•board
   ○ cardbo•ard

2. ○ ve•lvet
   ○ vel•vet
   ○ velv•et

3. ○ wo•bble
   ○ wobb•le
   ○ wob•ble

4. ○ ce•llar
   ○ cel•lar
   ○ cell•ar

5. ○ ca•ptive
   ○ cap•tive
   ○ capt•ive

6. ○ di•rect
   ○ dir•ect
   ○ dire•ct

7. ○ cot•tage
   ○ cott•age
   ○ cotta•ge

8. ○ wa•lrus
   ○ walr•us
   ○ wal•rus

9. ○ wrink•le
   ○ wri•nkle
   ○ wrin•kle

10. ○ cent•ral
    ○ cen•tral
    ○ ce•ntral

11. ○ di•sturb
    ○ dis•turb
    ○ dist•urb

12. ○ ba•rrel
    ○ bar•rel
    ○ barr•el

13. ○ fan•cy
    ○ fa•ncy
    ○ fanc•y

14. ○ wa•ter•fall
    ○ wat•erf•all
    ○ wa•terf•all

15. ○ fe•llow
    ○ fel•low
    ○ fell•ow

16. ○ be•have
    ○ beh•ave
    ○ behav•e

17. ○ a•ppear
    ○ ap•pear
    ○ app•ear

18. ○ clo•set
    ○ close•t
    ○ clos•et

Name _____

DIRECTIONS:
Read each group of words. Mark the one that is **not** spelled correctly.

1. ○ able
   ○ anyone
   ○ beside
   ○ buny
   ○ clap

2. ○ deside
   ○ eight
   ○ five
   ○ golden
   ○ hundred

3. ○ lay
   ○ meant
   ○ none
   ○ pen
   ○ probabbly

4. ○ root
   ○ she'll
   ○ somhow
   ○ tie
   ○ village

5. ○ wemen
   ○ zoom
   ○ wolf
   ○ vegetable
   ○ tickle

6. ○ sudden
   ○ sold
   ○ she'd
   ○ rooster
   ○ prise

7. ○ peek
   ○ nod
   ○ medow
   ○ late
   ○ goat

8. ○ fit
   ○ egg
   ○ deare
   ○ circus
   ○ bunch

9. ○ bend
   ○ anymor
   ○ watch
   ○ someone
   ○ note

10. ○ hole
    ○ done
    ○ bark
    ○ trik
    ○ place

11. ○ into
    ○ put
    ○ turtle
    ○ becuase
    ○ drink

12. ○ horse
    ○ onle
    ○ soon
    ○ wet
    ○ anyway

13. ○ bet
    ○ burn
    ○ clasroom
    ○ deep
    ○ either

14. ○ flap
    ○ goodness
    ○ hung
    ○ lead
    ○ meassure

15. ○ noon
    ○ pensil
    ○ problem
    ○ rose
    ○ she's

19

Name _____

DIRECTIONS:
Read each group of words. Mark the one that is **not** spelled correctly.

1. ○ somewhere
    ○ suit
    ○ tite
    ○ vine
    ○ won

2. ○ yourself
    ○ woke
    ○ van
    ○ Thirsday
    ○ such

3. ○ soil
    ○ sharp
    ○ rouf
    ○ print
    ○ peanut

4. ○ nobody
    ○ matter
    ○ large
    ○ huge
    ○ givn

5. ○ fishermen
    ○ editor
    ○ daitime
    ○ circle
    ○ bump

6. ○ bench
    ○ anybody
    ○ was'nt
    ○ someday
    ○ nose

7. ○ holde
    ○ doesn't
    ○ bake
    ○ tree
    ○ pick

8. ○ just
    ○ rabbitt
    ○ two
    ○ been
    ○ drove

9. ○ hungry
    ○ our
    ○ sorry
    ○ what
    ○ anewhere

10. ○ between
    ○ bush
    ○ clay
    ○ deer
    ○ elefant

11. ○ flach
    ○ gotten
    ○ hunt
    ○ leaf
    ○ meat

12. ○ north
    ○ penny
    ○ promise
    ○ rouff
    ○ sheet

13. ○ son
    ○ sumer
    ○ till
    ○ visit
    ○ wonder

14. ○ young
    ○ wize
    ○ valley
    ○ thunder
    ○ stuff

15. ○ soft
    ○ share
    ○ roller
    ○ prinse
    ○ pea

Name _____

DIRECTIONS:
Read each group of words. Mark the one that is **not** spelled correctly.

1. ○ nine
    ○ mask
    ○ lap
    ○ hug
    ○ gaint

2. ○ finish
    ○ edje
    ○ daylight
    ○ choose
    ○ built

3. ○ belt
    ○ answer
    ○ use
    ○ snow
    ○ noyse

4. ○ high
    ○ doctor
    ○ ate
    ○ top
    ○ poeple

5. ○ pat
    ○ took
    ○ aroind
    ○ dinner
    ○ herself

6. ○ nice
    ○ snake
    ○ untill
    ○ angry
    ○ below

7. ○ beyond
    ○ buzy
    ○ clear
    ○ desk
    ○ elevator

8. ○ flat
    ○ grab
    ○ huntor
    ○ lean
    ○ meet

9. ○ notice
    ○ pepper
    ○ proude
    ○ round
    ○ shell

10. ○ soup
     ○ Sunday
     ○ tinkle
     ○ voyce
     ○ wonderful

11. ○ you've
     ○ wire
     ○ upstairs
     ○ thump
     ○ stroong

12. ○ sock
     ○ shape
     ○ roll
     ○ pretind
     ○ pay

13. ○ newspapper
     ○ marry
     ○ language
     ○ howl
     ○ ghost

14. ○ finger
     ○ eaten
     ○ daugter
     ○ chirp
     ○ buildings

15. ○ belong
     ○ allso
     ○ smiled
     ○ never
     ○ zoo

Name _____

DIRECTIONS:
Read each group of words. Mark the one that is **not** spelled correctly.

1. ○ helpper
    ○ dark
    ○ aren't
    ○ today
    ○ park

2. ○ lake
    ○ ran
    ○ us
    ○ beggin
    ○ ever

3. ○ Iv'e
    ○ paint
    ○ squirrel
    ○ while
    ○ apartment

4. ○ bill
    ○ buter
    ○ clever
    ○ detective
    ○ else

5. ○ flew
    ○ grade
    ○ hurry
    ○ leep
    ○ melt

6. ○ nowwhere
    ○ perfect
    ○ prove
    ○ row
    ○ shine

7. ○ space
    ○ sunny
    ○ tiptoe
    ○ waggon
    ○ wool

8. ○ you'll
    ○ winner
    ○ upside
    ○ thumbe
    ○ stripe

9. ○ soap
    ○ shall
    ○ rode
    ○ press
    ○ paaw

10. ○ net
    ○ marcket
    ○ land
    ○ hour
    ○ graph

11. ○ final
    ○ eazy
    ○ dash
    ○ chin
    ○ build

12. ○ bell
    ○ already
    ○ tirn
    ○ smile
    ○ near

13. ○ heard
    ○ dance
    ○ apple
    ○ three
    ○ papper

14. ○ last
    ○ road
    ○ very
    ○ being
    ○ everone

15. ○ inside
    ○ pan
    ○ staind
    ○ white
    ○ arm

Name _____

DIRECTIONS:
Read each group of words. Mark the one that is **not** spelled correctly.

1. ○ blackbery
   ○ butterfly
   ○ click
   ○ die
   ○ elves

2. ○ flip
   ○ grandfather
   ○ I'd
   ○ leern
   ○ meow

3. ○ number
   ○ person
   ○ puff
   ○ rub
   ○ shiney

4. ○ spaceship
   ○ super
   ○ tood
   ○ wake
   ○ world

5. ○ yo'ud
   ○ wink
   ○ upset
   ○ throw
   ○ string

6. ○ sniff
   ○ shake
   ○ robber
   ○ present
   ○ pathe

7. ○ nest
   ○ mark
   ○ lady
   ○ hospital
   ○ gease

8. ○ fight
   ○ east
   ○ dandelion
   ○ child
   ○ bugg

9. ○ beleive
   ○ almost
   ○ try
   ○ smell
   ○ named

10. ○ hear
    ○ cri
    ○ anything
    ○ thought
    ○ over

11. ○ laugh
    ○ rock
    ○ wait
    ○ best
    ○ evereything

12. ○ isnt
    ○ part
    ○ star
    ○ wind
    ○ arrow

13. ○ blanket
    ○ climb
    ○ button
    ○ diferent
    ○ empty

14. ○ float
    ○ grandmoher
    ○ ice
    ○ leather
    ○ message

15. ○ nut
    ○ phone
    ○ pull
    ○ rouler
    ○ ship

Name _____

DIRECTIONS:
Read each group of words. Mark the one that is **not** spelled correctly.

1. ○ speak
    ○ supper
    ○ toast
    ○ wall
    ○ worme

2. ○ yet
    ○ wing
    ○ uppon
    ○ throughout
    ○ strike

3. ○ sneaker
    ○ shaddow
    ○ roar
    ○ practice
    ○ patch

4. ○ neiter
    ○ march
    ○ ladder
    ○ hose
    ○ gather

5. ○ feild
    ○ earth
    ○ damp
    ○ chief
    ○ brush

6. ○ behind
    ○ alley
    ○ trip
    ○ six
    ○ miself

7. ○ he's
    ○ could'nt
    ○ ant
    ○ there
    ○ or

8. ○ liked
    ○ sade
    ○ walk
    ○ better
    ○ everywhere

9. ○ jay
    ○ party
    ○ start
    ○ wintter
    ○ art

10. ○ bleew
    ○ buy
    ○ clock
    ○ dig
    ○ enemy

11. ○ flood
    ○ gray
    ○ idea
    ○ led
    ○ mett

12. ○ o'clock
    ○ piano
    ○ puppy
    ○ runer
    ○ shirt

13. ○ specal
    ○ suppose
    ○ toe
    ○ wander
    ○ worn

14. ○ year
    ○ win
    ○ untye
    ○ through
    ○ stretch

15. ○ snap
    ○ shaep
    ○ river
    ○ pour
    ○ paste

DIRECTIONS:
Read each group of words. Mark the one that is **not** spelled correctly.

1. ○ neighbor
   ○ map
   ○ known
   ○ horn
   ○ gat

2. ○ few
   ○ eirly
   ○ daddy
   ○ chicken
   ○ brought

3. ○ before
   ○ alike
   ○ tried
   ○ sisster
   ○ moved

4. ○ head
   ○ country
   ○ aney
   ○ think
   ○ other

5. ○ lion
   ○ same
   ○ was
   ○ bicke
   ○ eye

6. ○ keep
   ○ pickture
   ○ stay
   ○ wish
   ○ artist

7. ○ blok
   ○ cage
   ○ cloth
   ○ dine
   ○ enough

8. ○ flour
   ○ growl
   ○ important
   ○ leeft
   ○ mice

9. ○ osean
   ○ picnic
   ○ purple
   ○ rush
   ○ shook

10. ○ spell
    ○ swam
    ○ tommorow
    ○ warm
    ○ worry

11. ○ yard
    ○ wiffe
    ○ unhappy
    ○ though
    ○ straw

12. ○ smoke
    ○ seven
    ○ ring
    ○ pottato
    ○ past

13. ○ neck
    ○ lying
    ○ knot
    ○ hope
    ○ gardan

14. ○ fence
    ○ ear
    ○ curl
    ○ chew
    ○ brooke

15. ○ bedtime
    ○ airplaine
    ○ train
    ○ sign
    ○ move

Name _____

DIRECTIONS:
Read each group of words. Mark the one that is **not** spelled correctly.

1. ○ hand
   ○ cook
   ○ anather
   ○ then
   ○ open

2. ○ live
   ○ sat
   ○ water
   ○ bithday
   ○ face

3. ○ kind
   ○ plan
   ○ step
   ○ without
   ○ assleep

4. ○ bloom
   ○ camp
   ○ cornor
   ○ dirt
   ○ enter

5. ○ fold
   ○ frown
   ○ indede
   ○ lemon
   ○ middle

6. ○ ofice
   ○ pie
   ○ purr
   ○ rustle
   ○ shoot

7. ○ spend
   ○ sweete
   ○ tool
   ○ wash
   ○ worth

8. ○ wrote
   ○ wide
   ○ understood
   ○ third
   ○ stranjer

9. ○ silly
   ○ set
   ○ rid
   ○ pokket
   ○ pass

10. ○ nearby
    ○ main
    ○ knoock
    ○ honey
    ○ garbage

11. ○ felt
    ○ dust
    ○ cup
    ○ chest
    ○ brocken

12. ○ blow
    ○ kandle
    ○ clue
    ○ dish
    ○ evening

13. ○ follow
    ○ hapen
    ○ indoor
    ○ lesson
    ○ mile

14. ○ often
    ○ pile
    ○ quak
    ○ safe
    ○ short

15. ○ spent
    ○ swing
    ○ toss
    ○ wave
    ○ would'nt

Name _____

DIRECTIONS:
Read each group of words. Mark the one that is **not** spelled correctly.

1. ○ writen
   ○ whole
   ○ understand
   ○ thin
   ○ strange

2. ○ smart
   ○ sentnce
   ○ rich
   ○ porch
   ○ parrot

3. ○ nail
   ○ majic
   ○ knee
   ○ hit
   ○ gallop

4. ○ feelings
   ○ durning
   ○ crow
   ○ cherry
   ○ broke

5. ○ baord
   ○ candy
   ○ copy
   ○ dive
   ○ explain

6. ○ fool
   ○ hate
   ○ intrest
   ○ lick
   ○ miller

7. ○ liberry
   ○ instead
   ○ key
   ○ lunchroom
   ○ junk

8. ○ oil
   ○ pilow
   ○ queen
   ○ sail
   ○ shot

9. ○ spill
   ○ swung
   ○ touch
   ○ welcom
   ○ write

10. ○ whistle
    ○ truth
    ○ tent
    ○ stomak
    ○ size

11. ○ seek
    ○ reach
    ○ ponny
    ○ rainbow
    ○ ranch

12. ○ mouth
    ○ luck
    ○ jar
    ○ Fryday
    ○ hidden

13. ○ fear
    ○ favorite
    ○ change
    ○ cowboy
    ○ brase

14. ○ beach
    ○ afriad
    ○ baby
    ○ backyard
    ○ fresh

15. ○ joke
    ○ drive
    ○ crake
    ○ hammer
    ○ forget

Name _____

DIRECTIONS:
Read the sentences and choices below. Mark the word or phrase that means almost the same thing as the word or phrase that is underlined in the sentence.

1. I worked very hard and now my muscles <u>ache</u>.

   ○ **are soft**
   ○ **smell**
   ○ **are sore**

2. I want to own a large house when I am an <u>adult</u>.

   ○ **teenager**
   ○ **grown-up**
   ○ **doctor**

3. I will <u>aid</u> you in your search for your missing dog.

   ○ **call**
   ○ **find**
   ○ **help**

4. The warning bell let us know it was time to leave the ship.

   ○ **loud**
   ○ **alarm**
   ○ **captain's**

5. Please <u>allow</u> me to carry that heavy box for you.

   ○ **let**
   ○ **help**
   ○ **watch**

5. Is this the <u>actual</u> chair in which Abraham Lincoln sat?

   ○ **only**
   ○ **real**
   ○ **pretty**

7. Joe will read the book now and answer the questions <u>afterward</u>.

   ○ **first**
   ○ **tomorrow**
   ○ **later**

8. My <u>aim</u> is to be the best football player in this school!

   ○ **goal**
   ○ **shot**
   ○ **fast**

9. My great grandmother is 101 and still <u>alive</u>!

   ○ **dancing**
   ○ **happy**
   ○ **living**

10. The loose dog did not <u>appear</u> to be coming any closer.

   ○ **want**
   ○ **seem**
   ○ **run**

Name _____

Name _____

Skill: Synonyms—Test 2

DIRECTIONS:
Read the sentences and choices below. Mark the word or phrase that means almost the same thing as the word or phrase that is underlined in the sentence.

1. I could hear the train coming as I <u>approached</u> the tracks.

   ○ backed away from
   ○ looked at
   ○ neared

2. The <u>author</u> of this book is a friend of mine.

   ○ artist
   ○ writer
   ○ owner

3. Which <u>street</u> do I take to get to your house?

   ○ bus
   ○ turn
   ○ road

4. I do not want to <u>battle</u> with you.

   ○ eat
   ○ play
   ○ fight

5. Is that a <u>beetle</u> under that leaf?

   ○ rock
   ○ snake
   ○ bug

6. At what time did you <u>arrive</u>?

   ○ leave
   ○ come
   ○ get up

7. In <u>autumn</u>, the leaves turn red and yellow.

   ○ fall
   ○ spring
   ○ a month

8. I feel <u>awful</u> because I broke your baseball bat.

   ○ silly
   ○ glad
   ○ bad

9. The biggest <u>beast</u> in the zoo was the elephant.

   ○ animal
   ○ show
   ○ surprise

10. I <u>beg</u> you to let me have a pet parrot!

   ○ want
   ○ ask
   ○ tell

DIRECTIONS:
Read the sentences and choices below. Mark the word or phrase that means almost the same thing as the word or phrase that is underlined in the sentence.

1. Can you see what is <u>beneath</u> that pile of boxes?

   ○ in
   ○ under
   ○ behind

2. Joel likes to <u>boast</u> about all his first place ribbons and medals.

   ○ brag
   ○ tell
   ○ flash

3. <u>Brake</u> the car when you come to a corner.

   ○ hurry
   ○ start
   ○ stop

4. Dad asked Jack to <u>cut</u> down that old oak tree in the yard.

   ○ push
   ○ chop
   ○ knock

5. Nan will <u>creep</u> across the floor and scare Jane.

   ○ sweep
   ○ dash
   ○ crawl

6. The <u>blaze</u> burned the whole store before it was put it out.

   ○ sun
   ○ heat
   ○ fire

7. The boxes were <u>bound</u> tightly and I couldn't open any of them.

   ○ piled
   ○ wrapped
   ○ pushed

8. <u>Cast</u> your fishing line into that deep water under the bridge.

   ○ throw
   ○ drop
   ○ trim

9. Can Sue <u>complete</u> her paper by next Tuesday?

   ○ hand in
   ○ start
   ○ finish

10. That job was not so <u>difficult</u> to do!

    ○ easy
    ○ hard
    ○ awful

Name _____

DIRECTIONS:
Read the sentences and choices below. Mark the word or phrase that means almost the same thing as the word or phrase that is underlined in the sentence.

1. There are <u>a dozen</u> eggs in the bowl.

   ○ cracked
   ○ twelve
   ○ broken

2. I was so surprised, I thought I might <u>pass out</u>!

   ○ yell
   ○ freeze
   ○ faint

3. We could see the new car <u>gleaming</u> in the parking lot.

   ○ shining
   ○ running
   ○ driving

4. We used a <u>hollow</u> tube for the experiment.

   ○ round
   ○ straw
   ○ empty

5. Which jar has the <u>least</u> amount of candy?

   ○ greatest
   ○ fattest
   ○ smallest

6. Mom can <u>dye</u> this white shirt an make it brown.

   ○ color
   ○ mess up
   ○ wash

7. Rosie <u>flung</u> the newspaper into the trash can.

   ○ carried
   ○ tossed
   ○ dumped

8. Bob is really a good <u>guy</u> because he is always helping people.

   ○ cat
   ○ man
   ○ female

9. I can tie my shoes <u>in an instant</u>!

   ○ tightly
   ○ slowly
   ○ quickly

10. The <u>motion</u> of the boat on the waves made me feel a little ill.

   ○ movement
   ○ sound
   ○ smell

Name _____

DIRECTIONS:
Read the sentences and choices below. Mark the word or phrase that means almost the same thing as the word or phrase that is underlined in the sentence.

1. Get the <u>oars</u> for the boat.

- ○ **sails**
- ○ **fishing poles**
- ○ **paddles**

2. We can carry the water in that small <u>bucket</u>.

- ○ **pail**
- ○ **glass**
- ○ **shovel**

3. Will you <u>consider</u> giving me your skates when you get new ones?

- ○ **promise**
- ○ **think about**
- ○ **throw away**

4. The room was <u>dim</u> and cold.

- ○ **dirty**
- ○ **freezing**
- ○ **unlit**

5. You sing the words to the song and I will <u>echo</u> you.

- ○ **watch**
- ○ **listen to**
- ○ **repeat**

6. Sally is a quiet and <u>timid</u> girl.

- ○ **tall**
- ○ **shy**
- ○ **clever**

7. I have a <u>task</u> to do before I can come out and play.

- ○ **chore**
- ○ **game**
- ○ **book**

8. That <u>crook</u> just took my purse!

- ○ **bird**
- ○ **gust of wind**
- ○ **thief**

9. Help me <u>drag</u> this box to the garage.

- ○ **carry**
- ○ **pull**
- ○ **unpack**

10. That jewel might look pretty, but it is <u>a fake</u>!

- ○ **not real**
- ○ **a lot of money**
- ○ **broken**

Name _____

DIRECTIONS:
Read the sentences and choices below. Mark the word or phrase that means almost the same thing as the word or phrase that is underlined in the sentence.

1. Be careful driving because it is a <u>misty</u> morning.

   ○ **foggy**
   ○ **dry**
   ○ **nice**

2. When I hold up my hand you must <u>halt</u>!

   ○ **begin**
   ○ **run**
   ○ **stop**

3. Did you <u>invent</u> this wonderful new toy?

   ○ **play with**
   ○ **make**
   ○ **unwrap**

4. I am hungry so I will <u>munch</u> these crackers for awhile.

   ○ **borrow**
   ○ **hold**
   ○ **chew**

5. The captain will <u>steer</u> the ship safely to the dock.

   ○ **tow**
   ○ **sink**
   ○ **drive**

6. Sharon peeked into the <u>gloom</u>, but could see nothing.

   ○ **water**
   ○ **darkness**
   ○ **sunshine**

7. There was an <u>awful</u> storm coming our way.

   ○ **terrible**
   ○ **huge**
   ○ **puffy**

8. If we keep the boat <u>level</u>, it won't tip over.

   ○ **even**
   ○ **empty**
   ○ **here**

9. I am tired and need to <u>pause</u> for a moment.

   ○ **sleep**
   ○ **wait**
   ○ **breathe**

10. What is that big <u>bundle</u> Kelly is carrying?

    ○ **package**
    ○ **sheet**
    ○ **tray**

Name _____

DIRECTIONS:
Read the sentences and choices below. Mark the word or phrase that means almost the same thing as the word or phrase that is underlined in the sentence.

1. These new cards did not cost me a <u>cent</u>!

   ○ **dollar**
   ○ **nickel**
   ○ **penny**

2. Will you <u>continue</u> working while I answer the telephone?

   ○ **quit**
   ○ **keep on**
   ○ **busy**

3. My <u>dime</u> fell out of my pocket and rolled across the floor.

   ○ **pencil**
   ○ **watch**
   ○ **ten cents**

4. Shut off the <u>engine</u> when you put in the gas.

   ○ **motor**
   ○ **wind**
   ○ **oven**

5. I felt very <u>foolish</u> carrying an umbrella on a sunny day!

   ○ **comfortable**
   ○ **hot**
   ○ **silly**

6. I began to <u>chuckle</u> when I heard the news.

   ○ **cry**
   ○ **laugh**
   ○ **frown**

7. Naomi <u>crushed</u> the flowers when she stuffed them in the bag.

   ○ **smashed**
   ○ **protected**
   ○ **cut**

8. The spook house was a <u>dreadful</u> place to spend the night!

   ○ **wonderful**
   ○ **awful**
   ○ **strange**

9. The answers to this test are either true or <u>false</u>.

   ○ **given**
   ○ **not true**
   ○ **correct**

10. Dad said to use <u>glue</u> to hold the sticks together.

    ○ **nails**
    ○ **paste**
    ○ **rope**

Name _____

DIRECTIONS:
Read the sentences and choices below. Mark the word or phrase that means almost the same thing as the word or phrase that is underlined in the sentence.

1. Frank is the <u>champion</u> marble player in our club.

   ○ **best**
   ○ **worst**
   ○ **oldest**

2. Can you <u>discover</u> the answer to my question?

   ○ **work**
   ○ **tell**
   ○ **find**

3. Did you <u>enjoy</u> the movie?

   ○ **watch**
   ○ **go to**
   ○ **like**

4. Katrina wore a beautiful <u>gown</u> to the dance.

   ○ **crown**
   ○ **dress**
   ○ **coat**

5. The bee will not <u>harm</u> you if you stand still.

   ○ **hurt**
   ○ **buzz**
   ○ **scare**

6. You could hear the school bell <u>ring</u> two blocks away.

   ○ **circle**
   ○ **clang**
   ○ **shout**

7. The boat began to <u>drift</u> away because we didn't tie it to the

   ○ **wander**
   ○ **wonder**
   ○ **row**

8. The child was <u>fearful</u> that his mother was leaving.

   ○ **afraid**
   ○ **yelling**
   ○ **happy**

9. The hunter lived in a small <u>cottage</u> in the woods.

   ○ **place**
   ○ **tent**
   ○ **cabin**

10. Chrissy likes to <u>chatter</u> too much!

    ○ **eat**
    ○ **talk**
    ○ **play**

Name _____

DIRECTIONS:
Read the sentences and choices below. Mark the word or phrase that means almost the same thing as the word or phrase that is underlined in the sentence.

---

1. The clothesline began to <u>droop</u> and the clothes got dirty.

   ○ **break**
   ○ **sag**
   ○ **bounce**

2. Will you please <u>clip</u> the bushes by the front sidewalk?

   ○ **shape**
   ○ **water**
   ○ **trim**

3. An <u>enormous</u> storm cloud was headed toward the lake.

   ○ **dark**
   ○ **scary**
   ○ **huge**

4. Will you please <u>fetch</u> me a cool glass of water?

   ○ **throw**
   ○ **get**
   ○ **drink**

5. You may have <u>a couple</u> of those cookies after school.

   ○ **five**
   ○ **two**
   ○ **ten**

6. The bird built a <u>snug</u> nest for her seven blue eggs.

   ○ **cozy**
   ○ **high**
   ○ **big**

7. We waded in the <u>stream</u> to cool our feet.

   ○ **creek**
   ○ **shade**
   ○ **tall grass**

8. Father <u>commanded</u> me to pick up the tools I had been using.

   ○ **asked**
   ○ **ordered**
   ○ **begged**

9. We waited until <u>dawn</u> before leaving the house.

   ○ **evening**
   ○ **midnight**
   ○ **morning**

10. Do you have a good <u>grip</u> on the box so it won't fall?

    ○ **hold**
    ○ **ribbon**
    ○ **knee**

Name _____

DIRECTIONS:
Read the sentences and choices below. Mark the word that means the opposite of the word that is underlined in the sentence.

1. I am sorry I broke the vase. It was an <u>accident</u>.

   ○ clumsy
   ○ on purpose
   ○ wrong

2. Let's go to the movie and eat <u>afterward</u>.

   ○ later
   ○ before
   ○ dinner

3. I was <u>alarmed</u> when I heard the door open.

   ○ upset
   ○ scared
   ○ calm

4. Please read this page <u>silently</u> then answer the questions.

   ○ to yourself
   ○ openly
   ○ aloud

5. That car is really <u>ancient</u>!

   ○ old
   ○ new
   ○ rusty

6. I have the <u>actual</u> ball used in the big game!

   ○ false
   ○ orange
   ○ signed

7. That <u>child</u> should not be standing in the street.

   ○ baby
   ○ boy
   ○ adult

8. I think that fish by the rock is <u>dead</u>.

   ○ alive
   ○ not breathing
   ○ silver

9. I was <u>amazed</u> when I watched the magic show.

   ○ bored
   ○ happy
   ○ scared

10. After a warm shower, I felt <u>terrific</u>!

    ○ comfortable
    ○ clean
    ○ awful

Name _____

DIRECTIONS:
Read the sentences and choices below. Mark the word that means the opposite of the word that is underlined in the sentence.

1. Do you think these drapes will darken the room?

    ○ shade
    ○ cover
    ○ brighten

2. I am confused about what I should do next.

    ○ mixed up
    ○ sure
    ○ afraid

3. That car is enormous!

    ○ huge
    ○ shiny
    ○ tiny

4. Peter began to frown when it started to rain.

    ○ grin
    ○ worry
    ○ grow

5. Did the dog uncover that bone in my backyard?

    ○ chew
    ○ dig up
    ○ bury

6. I will warm the chocolate before we put it on the cookies.

    ○ heat
    ○ chill
    ○ eat

7. Did you lose your book?

    ○ find
    ○ misplace
    ○ hide

8. Do you think the answer is true?

    ○ good
    ○ real
    ○ false

9. I slept when I heard the gentle rain falling on the roof.

    ○ napped
    ○ looked
    ○ awoke

10. Please continue when you hear the bell.

    ○ stop
    ○ go on
    ○ begin

DIRECTIONS:
Read the sentences and choices below. Mark the word that means the opposite of the word that is underlined in the sentence.

1. I like to take a walk at <u>dawn</u> because the sky is so pretty.

   ○ **early**
   ○ **morning**
   ○ **dusk**

2. Janice wants a <u>fancy</u> dress for the party this Saturday.

   ○ **frilly**
   ○ **plain**
   ○ **pretty**

3. Harvey <u>happily</u> helped his mom bring in the heavy bags.

   ○ **joyfully**
   ○ **angrily**
   ○ **sweetly**

4. George was <u>anxious</u> about taking the test on Friday.

   ○ **scared**
   ○ **curious**
   ○ **calm**

5. Is this the <u>correct</u> way to fold a napkin?

   ○ **right**
   ○ **wrong**
   ○ **useful**

6. Please stand <u>at a distance</u> while I cut this log.

   ○ **over there**
   ○ **close**
   ○ **far away**

7. Is the ice cube <u>frozen</u>?

   ○ **melted**
   ○ **icy**
   ○ **square**

8. I can ride my bike <u>backward</u> over the bridge.

   ○ **slowly**
   ○ **quickly**
   ○ **forward**

9. The bird had many <u>colorful</u> feathers on its wings.

   ○ **dull**
   ○ **fluffy**
   ○ **bright**

10. Do not <u>drag</u> your bookbag across the floor.

   ○ **throw**
   ○ **push**
   ○ **lift**

Name _____

DIRECTIONS:
Read the sentences and choices below. Mark the word that means the opposite of the word that is underlined in the sentence.

1. Is this the <u>entrance</u> to the circus?

   ○ door
   ○ way in
   ○ exit

2. Are we any <u>closer</u>?

   ○ nearer
   ○ drier
   ○ further

3. The cups are on the shelf <u>above</u> the plates.

   ○ on top
   ○ beneath
   ○ over

4. Mark was <u>upset</u> when the dog sat on his lap.

   ○ angry
   ○ unhappy
   ○ comforted

5. The math problems for today were so <u>easy</u> to finish.

   ○ not hard
   ○ slow
   ○ difficult

6. Jose told his friend <u>farewell</u>.

   ○ goodbye
   ○ hello
   ○ good luck

7. I can't believe that you can just <u>disappear</u> like that!

   ○ show up
   ○ go away
   ○ hide

8. That is the biggest <u>mountain</u> I have ever seen.

   ○ hill
   ○ river
   ○ canyon

9. I will <u>creep</u> along the road until that strange car is gone.

   ○ speed
   ○ crawl
   ○ whisper

10. Ricky thought the play we saw was <u>wonderful</u>!

   ○ colorful
   ○ dreadful
   ○ very good

Name _____

DIRECTIONS:
Read the sentences and choices below. Mark the word that means the opposite of the word that is underlined in the sentence.

1. We each have <u>equal</u> stacks of baseball cards.

   ○ many
   ○ even
   ○ uneven

2. We can find the answer to pollution if we look to the <u>future</u>.

   ○ distance
   ○ next day
   ○ past

3. I can keep my arm <u>bent</u> for several hours.

   ○ straight
   ○ broken
   ○ crooked

4. I did not feel <u>comfortable</u> in the large chair.

   ○ easy
   ○ uneasy
   ○ warm

5. Can you <u>deliver</u> the package today?

   ○ bring
   ○ pick up
   ○ open

6. I can be <u>brave</u> when I am alone in a strange place.

   ○ fearful
   ○ fearless
   ○ strong

7. What time will you <u>arrive</u>?

   ○ come
   ○ meet
   ○ leave

8. Daniel wanted to <u>free</u> the whale.

   ○ let go
   ○ cost
   ○ capture

9. The cookie was <u>crisp</u> and tasty.

   ○ soggy
   ○ cracking
   ○ sweet

10. Sometimes Larry thinks he is really <u>smart</u>!

    ○ sharp
    ○ clever
    ○ dumb

DIRECTIONS:
Read the sentences and choices below. Mark the word that means the opposite of the word that is underlined in the sentence.

1. The girl in the red shirt is my friend.

   - ○ lady
   - ○ boy
   - ○ child

2. Ron was proud of the grade he got on his test.

   - ○ ashamed
   - ○ pleased
   - ○ careful

3. I beg you to give me back my book.

   - ○ ask
   - ○ dare
   - ○ command

4. Do not be so timid about meeting new people.

   - ○ afraid
   - ○ eager
   - ○ angry

5. Do you think that tiger in the cage is fierce?

   - ○ angry
   - ○ wild
   - ○ tame

6. I will stare when I see you.

   - ○ look away
   - ○ gaze
   - ○ blink

7. We keep our old clothes and toys in the cellar.

   - ○ basement
   - ○ closet
   - ○ attic

8. I think your new shoes are really cute!

   - ○ ugly
   - ○ old
   - ○ pretty

9. I am calm when I think about going on a trip to the ocean.

   - ○ excited
   - ○ quiet
   - ○ dreaming

10. I couldn't help but grin when I heard the news.

    - ○ smile
    - ○ frown
    - ○ growl

Name _____

DIRECTIONS:
Read the sentences and choices below. Mark the word that means the opposite of the word that is underlined in the sentence.

1. Who was the <u>loser</u> of the race?

   ○ worst
   ○ happiest
   ○ champion

2. You should keep a <u>damp</u> cloth on the sore until it feels better.

   ○ dry
   ○ wet
   ○ cold

3. Will you say some words that might <u>encourage</u> me?

   ○ help
   ○ discourage
   ○ support

4. This pillow is too <u>soft</u>!

   ○ comfortable
   ○ hard
   ○ difficult

5. I <u>love</u> the color of leaves in the autumn.

   ○ see
   ○ hate
   ○ like

6. A coin like this one is <u>rare</u>.

   ○ unusual
   ○ costly
   ○ common

7. I could see a <u>bright</u> light at the end of the tunnel.

   ○ shiny
   ○ dim
   ○ yellow

8. The surprise party we gave last night was a huge <u>success</u>.

   ○ smash
   ○ mess
   ○ failure

9. The <u>adult</u> quietly closed the door.

   ○ grown-up
   ○ man
   ○ youngster

10. I would like to <u>lend</u> a little help for this project.

   ○ send
   ○ give
   ○ borrow

Name _____

DIRECTIONS:
Read the sentences and choices below. Mark the word that means the opposite of the word that is underlined in the sentence.

1. We were <u>cheerful</u> when the game ended.

   ○ **sad**
   ○ **happy**
   ○ **yelling**

2. Is it <u>dangerous</u> to cross the street here?

   ○ **rare**
   ○ **safe**
   ○ **allowed**

3. I <u>hate</u> going to summer camp in the mountains.

   ○ **enjoy**
   ○ **don't like**
   ○ **miss**

4. Buying that car was a <u>foolish</u> thing to do.

   ○ **silly**
   ○ **useless**
   ○ **wise**

5. The <u>warmth</u> of the day felt good on my back.

   ○ **heat**
   ○ **coolness**
   ○ **sun**

6. Can you <u>complete</u> this project next week?

   ○ **finish**
   ○ **begin**
   ○ **do**

7. I am sure you will be <u>disappointed</u> if we watch that movie.

   ○ **angry**
   ○ **unhappy**
   ○ **pleased**

8. Is that a <u>real</u> beard your dad has?

   ○ **actual**
   ○ **fuzzy**
   ○ **fake**

9. You must speak in a <u>gentle</u> way if you expect your dog to listen.

   ○ **friendly**
   ○ **soft**
   ○ **gruff**

10. The hamburger was <u>tough</u> to chew.

    ○ **difficult**
    ○ **hard**
    ○ **easy**

Name _____

DIRECTIONS:
Read the sentences and choices below. Mark the word that means the opposite of the word that is underlined in the sentence.

1. Your name sounds <u>familiar</u> to me.

   ○ **common**
   ○ **usual**
   ○ **strange**

2. Mark tried to <u>capture</u> the wild cat.

   ○ **chase away**
   ○ **trap**
   ○ **set free**

3. I can <u>create</u> a whole city in my sandbox.

   ○ **build**
   ○ **destroy**
   ○ **pile**

4. That orange is very <u>juicy</u>!

   ○ **dry**
   ○ **wet**
   ○ **tasty**

5. I am <u>prepared</u> to give my report in class today.

   ○ **thankful**
   ○ **not ready**
   ○ **going**

6. I <u>awaken</u> at eight each day.

   ○ **sleep**
   ○ **get up**
   ○ **stretch**

7. Will you <u>fasten</u> the latch on the window?

   ○ **open**
   ○ **design**
   ○ **close**

8. I <u>depend on</u> my sister to make my bed.

   ○ **force**
   ○ **want**
   ○ **don't need**

9. Brian was a <u>naughty</u> boy today.

   ○ **good**
   ○ **bad**
   ○ **silly**

10. The sleeve of my jacket is <u>torn</u>.

   ○ **ripped**
   ○ **ragged**
   ○ **mended**

DIRECTIONS:
Read the first part of each sentence and look at the underlined word or words. Choose the word or phrase that means about the same thing as the underlined word or phrase. Mark the correct answer.

1. A word that means to <u>pull on sharply</u> is…

   ○ **push**
   ○ **yank**
   ○ **haul**

2. To <u>believe that someone is honest, fair, and true</u> means…

   ○ **like**
   ○ **protect**
   ○ **trust**

3. A person who <u>will not give in or change</u> his mind is…

   ○ **smart**
   ○ **daydreaming**
   ○ **stubborn**

4. The word <u>simple</u> means…

   ○ **easy**
   ○ **difficult**
   ○ **welcome**

5. A person who <u>throws an angry fit</u> is in a…

   ○ **carriage**
   ○ **emergency**
   ○ **rage**

6. To <u>take something off</u> a truck or ship is to…

   ○ **load**
   ○ **erase**
   ○ **unload**

7. Another word for <u>chore or job</u> is…

   ○ **task**
   ○ **test**
   ○ **declare**

8. A person who <u>fights for a cause</u> is a …

   ○ **visitor**
   ○ **friend**
   ○ **soldier**

9. To <u>save someone from danger</u> is to …

   ○ **calm**
   ○ **rescue**
   ○ **fault**

10. When you <u>take tiny bites</u> of your food you …

   ○ **nibble**
   ○ **delight**
   ○ **split**

Name _____

DIRECTIONS:
Read the first part of each sentence and look at the underlined word or words. Choose the word or phrase that means about the same thing as the underlined word or phrase. Mark the correct answer.

1. Another word for <u>partner</u> is…

   ○ self
   ○ passenger
   ○ mate

2. A <u>safe place for boats and ships</u> is a…

   ○ harbor
   ○ waterfall
   ○ figure

3. When two things are <u>even or level</u>, they are…

   ○ familiar
   ○ charming
   ○ equal

4. To <u>come closer</u> is to…

   ○ approach
   ○ choke
   ○ exclaim

5. A <u>small stream</u> of water is a…

   ○ layer
   ○ tickle
   ○ trickle

6. A <u>long trip</u> is called a…

   ○ thirst
   ○ symbol
   ○ journey

7. To <u>sparkle and shine</u> is to…

   ○ grumble
   ○ glitter
   ○ cast

8. A <u>person who buys something</u> is a…

   ○ customer
   ○ costume
   ○ cactus

9. Something that is <u>rare</u> is…

   ○ operate
   ○ unusual
   ○ immediate

10. Something <u>used to look at things that are far away</u> is a…

   ○ telephone
   ○ telescope
   ○ headlights

Name _____

DIRECTIONS:
Read the first part of each sentence and look at the underlined word or words. Choose the word or phrase that means about the same thing as the underlined word or phrase. Mark the correct answer.

1. To <u>take the bends out</u> of is to...

- ○ screech
- ○ position
- ○ straighten

2. To <u>say again</u> is to...

- ○ yawn
- ○ trace
- ○ repeat

3. We <u>wear these to bed</u> at night...

- ○ slippers
- ○ pajamas
- ○ sleeves

4. <u>Clothes that are being washed</u> are...

- ○ separate
- ○ liquid
- ○ laundry

5. To <u>hurt someone or something</u> is to do...

- ○ honor
- ○ cause
- ○ harm

6. When we <u>cuddle</u> something, we...

- ○ snuggle
- ○ serve
- ○ stoop

7. Something that is <u>rapid</u> is...

- ○ fast
- ○ old
- ○ slow

8. When you <u>do as you are told</u>, you...

- ○ roam
- ○ obey
- ○ strain

9. To <u>give a clue</u> is to...

- ○ hint
- ○ form
- ○ glance

10. A <u>group of birds</u> is called a...

- ○ business
- ○ flock
- ○ future

DIRECTIONS:
Read the first part of each sentence and look at the underlined word or words. Choose the word or phrase that means about the same thing as the underlined word or phrase. Mark the correct answer.

1. When you <u>give many details</u> about something you...

   ○ describe
   ○ rebel
   ○ cluster

2. What a balloon does when it <u>pops</u>...

   ○ secure
   ○ locate
   ○ burst

3. Something that is <u>as bad as it gets</u> is the...

   ○ request
   ○ worst
   ○ wept

4. To s<u>hake from fear or excitement</u> is to...

   ○ wheeze
   ○ tremble
   ○ spear

5. Something that is <u>excellent</u> is...

   ○ eerie
   ○ dainty
   ○ splendid

6. Things <u>put together into a set</u> make a...

   ○ complaint
   ○ collection
   ○ corral

7. Something that <u>covers and protects</u> us is...

   ○ shatter
   ○ mournful
   ○ armor

8. Something that is <u>common or everyday</u> is...

   ○ usual
   ○ wisdom
   ○ speck

9. When you really <u>want something to drink</u>, you have...

   ○ tradition
   ○ stake
   ○ thirst

10. A person who is <u>thin</u> is usually called...

   ○ slim
   ○ definite
   ○ inspector

Name _____

DIRECTIONS:
Read the first part of each sentence and look at the underlined word or words. Choose the word or phrase that means about the same thing as the underlined word or phrase. Mark the correct answer.

1. To <u>wash or clean by rubbing hard</u> is to...
   - ○ dimple
   - ○ crumble
   - ○ scrub

2. When you <u>get something</u> you ...
   - ○ reappear
   - ○ navigate
   - ○ receive

3. Two things that are <u>completely different</u> are called...
   - ○ onward
   - ○ opposite
   - ○ mischief

4. Anything that <u>happened before now</u> is the...
   - ○ future
   - ○ past
   - ○ native

5. To <u>make a person do something he doesn't want to do</u> is to...
   - ○ force
   - ○ outwit
   - ○ link

6. When you <u>stay behind</u> you...
   - ○ remain
   - ○ hitch
   - ○ express

7. A <u>group of related sentences</u> is a...
   - ○ paragraph
   - ○ sniffle
   - ○ mission

8. The <u>smallest amount</u> is the...
   - ○ rate
   - ○ mutter
   - ○ least

9. To be <u>thankful</u> is to be...
   - ○ necessary
   - ○ sloppy
   - ○ grateful

10. A <u>book that lists the meaning</u> of words is a...
    - ○ marvel
    - ○ represent
    - ○ dictionary

Name _____

DIRECTIONS:
Read the first part of each sentence and look at the underlined word or words. Choose the word or phrase that means about the same thing as the underlined word or phrase. Mark the correct answer.

1. To <u>order</u> someone to do something is a...

   ○ **trough**
   ○ **command**
   ○ **suggestion**

2. A <u>person who helps another</u> is an...

   ○ **accident**
   ○ **adult**
   ○ **assistant**

3. Something that is <u>very expensive or dear</u> to you is a...

   ○ **centimeter**
   ○ **assembly**
   ○ **treasure**

4. To <u>splash</u> drops of water is to...

   ○ **shed**
   ○ **combine**
   ○ **sprinkle**

5. A <u>part</u> of something is a...

   ○ **cloak**
   ○ **section**
   ○ **fashion**

6. A person who is <u>unable to see</u> is...

   ○ **solemn**
   ○ **blind**
   ○ **witness**

7. To <u>shake back and forth</u>, almost falling down is to...

   ○ **overflow**
   ○ **concern**
   ○ **wobble**

8. A person who is <u>quiet and shy</u> is often called...

   ○ **timid**
   ○ **constant**
   ○ **rumpled**

9. A dog or cat with <u>long, uneven hair</u> is...

   ○ **countless**
   ○ **sensible**
   ○ **shaggy**

10. When you <u>say you will not do something</u>, you...

    ○ **refuse**
    ○ **direct**
    ○ **crouch**

Name _____

DIRECTIONS:
Read the first part of each sentence and look at the underlined word or words. Choose the word or phrase that means about the same thing as the underlined word or phrase. Mark the correct answer.

1. To <u>get ready</u> is to...

   ○ prepare
   ○ invent
   ○ extend

2. When you are <u>very unhappy</u> you are...

   ○ honest
   ○ miserable
   ○ darling

3. A <u>person who wants everything</u> and doesn't share is...

   ○ harmless
   ○ barefoot
   ○ greedy

4. A person who is very <u>devout</u> is...

   ○ faithful
   ○ disappointed
   ○ independent

5. To <u>watch and listen closely</u> is to give your...

   ○ attention
   ○ disgust
   ○ launch

6. A <u>short stop or break</u> is a...

   ○ kindness
   ○ jersey
   ○ pause

7. To be <u>flat or even</u> is...

   ○ humble
   ○ level
   ○ grim

8. A person who is the <u>best at what he does</u> is an...

   ○ expert
   ○ octopus
   ○ ingredient

9. A <u>child of your aunt or uncle</u> is your...

   ○ brother
   ○ headache
   ○ cousin

10. A <u>stiff hair on the face of a cat or dog</u> is a...

   ○ whisper
   ○ whisker
   ○ gland

DIRECTIONS:
Read the first part of each sentence and look at the underlined word or words. Choose the word or phrase that means about the same thing as the underlined word or phrase. Mark the correct answer.

1. A person who is a <u>guest</u> is a...

   ○ tradition
   ○ volunteer
   ○ visitor

2. <u>Drops of water that fall from your skin</u> when you are hot are...

   ○ faucet
   ○ sweat
   ○ itch

3. To <u>wander without purpose</u> is to...

   ○ horrify
   ○ display
   ○ roam

4. A person who is <u>well liked</u> by many other people is...

   ○ advanced
   ○ popular
   ○ painful

5. <u>As far as you can go</u> is the...

   ○ current
   ○ deserve
   ○ limit

6. <u>People, cars, trucks, and buses coming and going</u> are...

   ○ haul
   ○ traffic
   ○ desperate

7. Something that is <u>not very deep</u> is...

   ○ shallow
   ○ rhythmic
   ○ lagoon

8. To <u>stop something from happening</u> is to...

   ○ caress
   ○ conduct
   ○ prevent

9. Something <u>new and up to date</u> is...

   ○ antique
   ○ grizzly
   ○ modern

10. Something that is <u>not real</u> is...

   ○ imaginary
   ○ glossy
   ○ dignified

Name _____

DIRECTIONS:
Read the first part of each sentence and look at the underlined word or words. Choose the word or phrase that means about the same thing as the underlined word or phrase. Mark the correct answer.

1. Anything that has <u>not yet happened</u> is in the...
   - ○ household
   - ○ future
   - ○ dungeon

2. Something <u>far away</u> is in the...
   - ○ century
   - ○ coolness
   - ○ distance

3. The <u>person who writes</u> a paper or a book is the...
   - ○ disease
   - ○ hamster
   - ○ author

4. To <u>walk through shallow water</u> is to...
   - ○ haul
   - ○ shatter
   - ○ wade

5. To <u>talk in front of other people</u> is to give a...
   - ○ shriek
   - ○ savage
   - ○ speech

6. A <u>large meal</u> is a...
   - ○ freckle
   - ○ drill
   - ○ feast

7. A <u>person in a story</u> is a...
   - ○ character
   - ○ clump
   - ○ seller

8. <u>How much a person or thing weighs</u> is his...
   - ○ intend
   - ○ freight
   - ○ weight

9. When you <u>offer an idea</u>, you give a...
   - ○ prop
   - ○ major
   - ○ suggestion

10. A <u>puzzling question or problem</u> is a...
    - ○ riddle
    - ○ valve
    - ○ wrestler

DIRECTIONS:
Read each sentence and look at the underlined word or words. If there is no error in capitalization or punctuation, mark the answer "correct." If there is an error, choose the answer that has the correct capitalization and punctuation.

1. Susan lives in <u>new york</u>.

   ○ **correct**
   ○ **New York**
   ○ **New york**
   ○ **new York**

2. <u>what did the mailman</u> bring to the door?

   ○ **correct**
   ○ **what did the Mailman**
   ○ **What did the Mailman**
   ○ **What did the mailman**

3. Kelly will <u>sing and,</u> Peggy will dance.

   ○ **correct**
   ○ **sing, and**
   ○ **sing; and**
   ○ **sing. and**

4. It is almost dark. <u>we'd better hurry</u> home!

   ○ **correct**
   ○ **W'ed better hurry**
   ○ **We'd Better hurry**
   ○ **We'd better hurry**

5. My favorite book is called <u>*The silver peach.*</u>

   ○ **correct**
   ○ ***The Silver Peach***
   ○ ***the Silver Peach***
   ○ ***the silver peach***

6. What a surprise! How did you know it was just what I <u>wanted.</u>

   ○ **correct**
   ○ **wanted,**
   ○ **wanted?**
   ○ **Wanted.**

7. I used <u>red, green, and yellow</u> dots on my monster.

   ○ **correct**
   ○ **red green, and yellow**
   ○ **red, green, and, yellow**
   ○ **red, green and yellow,**

8. <u>Kevin's aunt</u> is coming to visit next week.

   ○ **correct**
   ○ **Kevins' aunt**
   ○ **Kevins's aunt**
   ○ **Kevins Aunt**

9. Jeff lives in <u>Detroit Michigan</u>.

   ○ **correct**
   ○ **Detroit, michigan**
   ○ **Detroit, Michigan**
   ○ **detroit, michigan**

10. Is today the day of <u>our picnic?</u>

   ○ **correct**
   ○ **our Picnic?**
   ○ **our picnic!**
   ○ **our picnic.**

DIRECTIONS:
Read each sentence and look at the underlined word or words. If there is no error in capitalization or punctuation, mark the answer "correct." If there is an error, choose the answer that has the correct capitalization and punctuation.

1. <u>when will we be</u> leaving for the airport?

   - ○ correct
   - ○ when will we, be
   - ○ When will, we be
   - ○ When will we be

2. <u>kevins dog</u> dug a huge hole under the fence!

   - ○ correct
   - ○ Kevins dog
   - ○ kevin's dog
   - ○ Kevin's dog

3. I went to <u>Washington, DC</u> with my parents.

   - ○ correct
   - ○ washington, d.c.
   - ○ Washington D.C.
   - ○ Washington, D.C.

4. <u>Fran and Billy</u> were surprised to see me at the party!

   - ○ correct
   - ○ Fran, and billy
   - ○ Fran and Billy,
   - ○ Fran and billy

5. My older brother goes to <u>woodlake middle school</u>.

   - ○ correct
   - ○ Woodlake middle school
   - ○ Woodlake Middle School
   - ○ Woodlake Middle, School

6. Peter asked <u>Mr Smith</u> to come to our school play.

   - ○ correct
   - ○ Mr. Smith
   - ○ mr. Smith
   - ○ Mr smith

7. Jay has a pet <u>parrot. And a</u> small brown rabbit.

   - ○ correct
   - ○ parrot and a
   - ○ parrot! And a
   - ○ parrot and, a

8. I put the <u>ornaments, lights, and star</u> on the tree.

   - ○ correct
   - ○ ornaments lights, and star
   - ○ ornaments lights and star
   - ○ ornaments, lights, and , star

9. It is time to go. <u>let's hurry, or we</u> will miss the train!

   - ○ correct
   - ○ Let's hurry or We
   - ○ Let's hurry, or we
   - ○ Let's, hurry or we

10. It looks like rain. Shall we take our umbrellas <u>to the park.</u>

   - ○ correct
   - ○ to the Park.
   - ○ to the park!
   - ○ to the park?

DIRECTIONS:
Read each sentence and look at the underlined word or words. If there is no error in capitalization or punctuation, mark the answer "correct." If there is an error, choose the answer that has the correct capitalization and punctuation.

1. Will you <u>come with us. I think</u> you will enjoy the journey.

   ○ **correct**
   ○ **come with us, I think**
   ○ **come with us? I think**
   ○ **come with us? i think**

2. <u>Jack's parents</u> took a three week trip to China last year.

   ○ **correct**
   ○ **Jacks parents**
   ○ **jack's parents**
   ○ **Jack's Parents**

3. <u>put the camera on</u> the top shelf so it won't get broken!

   ○ **correct**
   ○ **Put the Camera on**
   ○ **Put the camera on**
   ○ **Put the camera. On**

4. Are they here <u>yet? I would like to</u> meet them.

   ○ **correct**
   ○ **yet, I would like to**
   ○ **yet. I would like to**
   ○ **yet! I would, like to**

5. Have you ever read the book called <u>*come home tomorrow*</u>?

   ○ **correct**
   ○ *come home tomorrow* **!**
   ○ *Come home tomorrow* **?**
   ○ *Come Home Tomorrow* **?**

6. Ben lives on <u>hartman street</u>, near the bus stop.

   ○ **correct**
   ○ **hartman Street**
   ○ **Hartman street**
   ○ **Hartman Street**

7. <u>Betty, Jane, Cora and Patty</u> are coming to my party.

   ○ **correct**
   ○ **Betty, Jane, Cora, and Patty**
   ○ **Betty Jane, Cora and Patty**
   ○ **Betty, Jane, Cora, and Patty,**

8. <u>Havent</u> you finished your homework yet?

   ○ **correct**
   ○ **havent**
   ○ **Have'nt**
   ○ **Haven't**

9. <u>That Dinosaur is</u> my favorite one in the museum!

   ○ **correct**
   ○ **That dinosaur is**
   ○ **That Dinosaur, is**
   ○ **That dinosaur. Is**

10. <u>Miss silbert is a very</u> good teacher.

   ○ **correct**
   ○ **Miss Silbert is a very**
   ○ **Miss silbert, is a very**
   ○ **Miss Silbert, is a very**

Name _____ Skill: Capitalization and Punctuation—Test 4

DIRECTIONS:
Read each sentence and look at the underlined word or words. If there is no error in capitalization or punctuation, mark the answer "correct." If there is an error, choose the answer that has the correct capitalization and punctuation.

1. There were <u>six student's</u> in the room after lunch.

   ○ correct
   ○ six Student's
   ○ six students
   ○ six students'

2. <u>I did'nt know</u> that Jason and Steve are brothers!

   ○ correct
   ○ i didn't know
   ○ I didnt know
   ○ I didn't know

3. <u>Alice marie is</u> my best friend.

   ○ correct
   ○ Alice Marie is
   ○ Alice, Marie is
   ○ Alice, Marie, is

4. What time <u>is it? I</u> can't see the clock from here.

   ○ correct
   ○ is it, I
   ○ is it! I
   ○ is it? i

5. The bird is in <u>her nest I think</u> she has some eggs in there.

   ○ correct
   ○ her nest. I think
   ○ her nest; i think
   ○ her nest? I think

6. Did you know that <u>tomorrow is my tenth birthday!</u>

   ○ correct
   ○ tomorrow is my tenth birthday.
   ○ tomorrow, is my tenth Birthday!
   ○ tomorrow is my tenth birthday?

7. Ken will set the <u>table and</u> wash the dishes.

   ○ correct
   ○ table, and
   ○ table and,
   ○ table: and

8. <u>Joe, Tom, and Bill</u> want to play soccer after school.

   ○ correct
   ○ Joe, tom, and bill
   ○ Joe, Tom and Bill
   ○ Joe Tom and, Bill

9. Nancy has a cousin that lives in <u>Peidmont Oregon</u>.

   ○ correct
   ○ peidmont oregon.
   ○ Peidmont Oregon;
   ○ Peidmont, Oregon.

10. <u>Elly and craig</u> are building a club house today!

   ○ correct
   ○ elly and craig
   ○ elly and Craig
   ○ Elly and Craig

DIRECTIONS:
Read each sentence and look at the underlined word or words. If there is no error in capitalization or punctuation, mark the answer "correct." If there is an error, choose the answer that has the correct capitalization and punctuation.

1. I will have <u>pizza potato chips and cola</u> for lunch!
   - ○ **correct**
   - ○ pizza, potato, chips and cola
   - ○ pizza, potato chips, and cola
   - ○ pizza, potato chips, and cola,

2. Which dress do you think I should wear <u>to the dance?</u>
   - ○ **correct**
   - ○ **to the Dance?**
   - ○ **to the dance!**
   - ○ **to the dance.**

3. <u>This dictionary has</u> two words that are not spelled correctly!
   - ○ **correct**
   - ○ **This Dictionary has**
   - ○ **This Dictionary, has**
   - ○ **This dictionary, has**

4. I stood on the <u>golden gate bridge</u> in San Francisco!
   - ○ **correct**
   - ○ **Golden Gate Bridge**
   - ○ **Golden Gate bridge**
   - ○ **Golden gate bridge**

5. I don't like that <u>movie. Because it</u> frightens me too much!
   - ○ **correct**
   - ○ **movie because it**
   - ○ **movie because, it**
   - ○ **Movie. Because it**

6. <u>Main street is</u> usually in the center of a town or city.
   - ○ **correct**
   - ○ **Main street are**
   - ○ **Main Street is**
   - ○ **Main Street are**

7. <u>use glue, glitter, and silver</u> paint to make this beautiful picture frame.
   - ○ **correct**
   - ○ **Use glue glitter and silver**
   - ○ **Use glue, glitter and, silver**
   - ○ **Use glue, glitter, and silver**

8. Martha had a small <u>part in the play.</u>
   - ○ **correct**
   - ○ **part in the Play.**
   - ○ **part in the play?**
   - ○ **part, in the play.**

9. Cindy said that <u>Mindys letter</u> arrived in the mail today!
   - ○ **correct**
   - ○ **Mindys Letter**
   - ○ **Mindy's letter**
   - ○ **mindys' letter**

10. Do you think <u>your new Neighbor</u> has moved in yet?
    - ○ **correct**
    - ○ **Your new Neighbor**
    - ○ **your new, neighbor**
    - ○ **your new neighbor**

Name _____

DIRECTIONS:
Read each sentence and look at the underlined word or words. If there is no error in capitalization or punctuation, mark the answer "correct." If there is an error, choose the answer that has the correct capitalization and punctuation.

1. The prettiest flowers are <u>Roses and Tulips.</u>

   O **correct**
   O **Roses and Tulips?**
   O **roses and tulips.**
   O **Roses and tulips.**

2. <u>Meg and Tony hid</u> the treasure behind the stone wall.

   O **correct**
   O **Meg, and Tony**
   O **Meg, and tony**
   O **meg, and tony**

3. <u>Miss Snows third grade class</u> won the tug-of-war contest!

   O **correct**
   O **Miss Snow's Third grade class**
   O **Miss Snows Third Grade class**
   O **Miss Snow's third grade class**

4. Is that you under that <u>mask! I</u> couldn't tell who it was!

   O **correct**
   O **Mask! I**
   O **mask, I**
   O **mask? I**

5. Did you hear <u>what I just said!</u>

   O **correct**
   O **what i just said!**
   O **what I just said.**
   O **what I just said?**

6. <u>Harry and David is</u> my friends.

   O **correct**
   O **Harry and david is**
   O **Harry and david are**
   O **Harry and David are**

7. Do you live on <u>Elm street or Oak street?</u>

   O **correct**
   O **Elm street or Oak street.**
   O **Elm Street or Oak Street?**
   O **Elm Street or Oak Street,**

8. We had <u>roast turkey and stuffing</u> for dinner last night.

   O **correct**
   O **roast turkey, and stuffing**
   O **roast Turkey and stuffing**
   O **Roast Turkey, and stuffing**

9. We went to <u>Disney world for our</u> vacation last year.

   O **correct**
   O **disney world for Our**
   O **Disney World for Our**
   O **Disney World for our**

10. I asked <u>Amy, Susie, and Bonnie,</u> to come to my house today.

   O **correct**
   O **Amy Susie and Bonnie.**
   O **Amy, Susie, and Bonnie**
   O **Amy Susie, and Bonnie,**

DIRECTIONS:

Read each sentence and look at the underlined word or words. If there is no error in capitalization or punctuation, mark the answer "correct." If there is an error, choose the answer that has the correct capitalization and punctuation.

1. <u>Greenleaf ave</u> is the longest street in town.
   - ○ correct
   - ○ Greenleaf Ave.
   - ○ Greenleaf ave.
   - ○ greenleaf ave.

2. I will be careful <u>crossing the street.</u>
   - ○ correct
   - ○ crossing the Street!
   - ○ crossing the Street?
   - ○ crossing the street?

3. It is a windy <u>day in april. I think</u> I will fly a kite!
   - ○ correct
   - ○ day. In april I think
   - ○ day in April. I think
   - ○ day in April I think

4. The <u>young robin flew</u> across the sky.
   - ○ correct
   - ○ young Robin flew
   - ○ young, robin flew
   - ○ young robin. Flew

5. It is cold <u>outside all</u> the trees are bare.
   - ○ correct
   - ○ outside. All
   - ○ outside, all
   - ○ Outside. All

6. <u>we have</u> a new television!
   - ○ correct
   - ○ We Have
   - ○ we Have
   - ○ We have

7. Mom likes <u>to cook she cooks great</u> dinners!
   - ○ correct
   - ○ to. Cook she cooks great.
   - ○ to cook. She cooks great
   - ○ to cook she. Cooks great

8. My <u>grandmothers</u> picture is on the table in my bedroom.
   - ○ correct
   - ○ Grandmothers
   - ○ grandmother's
   - ○ Grandmothers'

9. The circus tent is <u>red, and yellow with blue</u> stripes.
   - ○ correct
   - ○ red and yellow, with blue,
   - ○ red, and yellow, with blue
   - ○ red and yellow with blue

10. Last <u>friday was</u> the first day of October.
    - ○ correct
    - ○ friday, was
    - ○ Friday Was
    - ○ Friday was

Name _____

DIRECTIONS:
Read each sentence and look at the underlined word or words. If there is no error in capitalization or punctuation, mark the answer "correct." If there is an error, choose the answer that has the correct capitalization and punctuation.

1. When will you <u>go to california.</u>

○ **correct**
○ **go to California?**
○ **go to california.**
○ **go to california?**

2. The mice did not hear the <u>cat's bell</u> in time!

○ **correct**
○ **cats bell**
○ **Cat's Bell**
○ **Cats bell**

3. Jim painted a picture of <u>leave's and flower's.</u>

○ **correct**
○ **leave and flower**
○ **leaves and flowers'**
○ **leaves and flowers**

4. I have a lot of fun when I stay with <u>aunt Phyllis.</u>

○ **correct**
○ **aunt phyllis**
○ **Aunt phyllis**
○ **Aunt Phyllis**

5. I have a red <u>car, chris</u> has a blue car.

○ **correct**
○ **car. chris**
○ **Car. Chris**
○ **car. Chris**

6. <u>Joe Tom and Frank</u> are in my class.

○ **correct**
○ **Joe, tom, and frank**
○ **Joe, Tom, and Frank**
○ **Joe Tom, and Frank**

7. My <u>brother and Sister</u> went to the store with our neighbor.

○ **correct**
○ **brother and sister**
○ **Brother and Sister**
○ **brother, and sister**

8. <u>The school bus</u> slipped on the muddy road.

○ **correct**
○ **The School bus**
○ **The School Bus**
○ **The school Bus**

9. The <u>bird's made a nest</u> in the top of that tree.

○ **correct**
○ **birds made a nest**
○ **birds' made a nest**
○ **Birds made a nest**

10. Did that elephant <u>just eat a peanut?</u>

○ **correct**
○ **just eat a peanut!**
○ **just eat. a peanut?**
○ **just eat a peanut.**

Name _____

DIRECTIONS:
Read each sentence and look at the underlined word or words. If there is no error in capitalization or punctuation, mark the answer "correct." If there is an error, choose the answer that has the correct capitalization and punctuation.

1. <u>many people like</u> to dance when the music plays.
   - ○ correct
   - ○ Many People like
   - ○ Many people. Like
   - ○ Many people like

2. We <u>walked, and walked</u> for many miles.
   - ○ correct
   - ○ walked, and walked,
   - ○ walked and walked
   - ○ walked: and walked

3. My <u>Horse and Monkey</u> are good friends!
   - ○ correct
   - ○ horse and monkey
   - ○ Horse, and monkey
   - ○ horse and monkey,

4. James would like to play in the <u>school band,</u>
   - ○ correct
   - ○ School Band.
   - ○ School band.
   - ○ school band.

5. Judy just read <u>*The Wind in the Willows*</u>.
   - ○ correct
   - ○ *the Wind In The Willows*
   - ○ *The Wind In The Willows*
   - ○ *the Wind in The willows*

6. The whale is one of the <u>largest Animals</u> in the world.
   - ○ correct
   - ○ Largest Animals
   - ○ largest animal
   - ○ largest animals

7. <u>Mr. Klein</u> is one of the nicest men I know!
   - ○ correct
   - ○ mr klein
   - ○ Mr. klein
   - ○ Mr. Klein.

8. The train had an <u>engine six cars and a</u> caboose!
   - ○ correct
   - ○ Engine six cars and a
   - ○ engine, six cars and a,
   - ○ engine, six cars, and a

9. Have you ever seen the <u>empire state building</u> in New York?
   - ○ correct
   - ○ Empire state building
   - ○ Empire State Building
   - ○ Empire state Building

10. <u>Wendys shoes</u> were covered in mud after the storm.
    - ○ correct
    - ○ Wendy's shoes
    - ○ Wendys' shoes
    - ○ Wendys shoe's

DIRECTIONS:
Read each sentence and look at the underlined word or words. If there is no error in capitalization or punctuation, mark the answer "correct." If there is an error, choose the answer that has the correct capitalization and punctuation.

1. My uncle lives in <u>Tampa Florida</u>.

   ○ correct
   ○ Tampa, Florida
   ○ tampa florida
   ○ Tampa; Florida

2. <u>The paper and paints'</u> are ready for art class.

   ○ correct
   ○ Paper and Paints
   ○ paper and paints
   ○ paper and paint's

3. <u>Mother and father</u> is a very good movie.

   ○ correct
   ○ Mother And Father
   ○ Mother and Father
   ○ mother and Father

4. Will it <u>rain? or will</u> it snow?

   ○ correct
   ○ Rain? Or will
   ○ rain! Or will
   ○ rain? Or will

5. Did you see the ending of the <u>race? Who won?</u>

   ○ correct
   ○ race! Who won!
   ○ race! Who won?
   ○ race. Who won?

6. Vera chose <u>silver, blue red, and green</u> as her four colors.

   ○ correct
   ○ silver blue, red, and green
   ○ silver, blue, red, and green
   ○ silver, blue, red, and, green

7. <u>Juan's sister</u> is only three years old.

   ○ correct
   ○ Juans sister
   ○ Juans Sister
   ○ Juans' sister

8. <u>Terry and i</u> are planning a picnic for next Saturday.

   ○ correct
   ○ terry and I
   ○ Terry and I
   ○ terry and i

9. This letter is addressed to <u>Dr. Paul J Keller</u>.

   ○ correct
   ○ Dr. Paul. J Keller
   ○ Dr Paul. J. Keller
   ○ Dr. Paul J. Keller

10. George will meet you on the steps of the <u>library next saturday morning</u>.

    ○ correct
    ○ library next Saturday morning
    ○ Library next Saturday morning
    ○ library next Saturday Morning

Name _____

DIRECTIONS:
Read each story, then read each question. Read all the answers, then mark the space for the answer you think is right. Mark NH (not here) if the answer can't be figured out from the given information.

Sarah took the scissors and tape from the desk. She chose a roll of blue wrapping paper with silver stars on it. She slipped into her brother's room and took his crayons and glue. Sarah quietly went to her room and closed the door. Sarah took a large box from her closet. It was a model ship for Danny's birthday. Sarah had saved her money for three weeks to buy this present. She knew Danny would like it. He had lots of models, but none like this! Sarah wrapped the box and hid it in the closet.

1. Where did Sarah find the glue and crayons?
   - ○ in the desk
   - ○ in her room
   - ○ in her brother's room
   - ○ NH

2. What color was the wrapping paper?
   - ○ green with red hearts
   - ○ blue with silver stars
   - ○ silver with blue stars
   - ○ NH

3. Why was Sarah being so quiet?
   - ○ she didn't feel well
   - ○ she was hiding
   - ○ she wanted to surprise Danny
   - ○ NH

4. How did Sarah know that Danny would like her present?
   - ○ she likes Danny
   - ○ Danny likes models
   - ○ Danny likes crayons and glue
   - ○ NH

5. What is the name of Sarah's brother?
   - ○ Mark
   - ○ Danny
   - ○ Frank
   - ○ NH

6. When will it be Danny's birthday?
   - ○ today
   - ○ June 3
   - ○ in three weeks
   - ○ NH

7. Why did Sarah hide the present after she had wrapped it?
   - ○ it is a surprise
   - ○ she didn't like how it looked
   - ○ Sarah wanted the model herself
   - ○ NH

8. What words from the story help you know that Sarah is trying to keep a secret?
   - ○ scissors, crayons, closed
   - ○ saved, models, wrapped
   - ○ slipped, quietly, hid
   - ○ NH

Name _____

DIRECTIONS:
Read each story, then read each question. Read all the answers, then mark the space for the answer you think is right. Mark NH (not here) if the answer can't be figured out from the given information.

Kerry poured water into the bottle and added ice, then screwed the lid on tightly. He did not want the bottle to leak on this trip! He opened a large paper bag and put the water bottle inside. Kerry made four peanut butter sandwiches and wrapped them carefully. Would a jar of pickles travel well? Kerry decided they would not. Instead, he found a bag of chips and tossed them into the bag. Three bananas, two apples, and some carrots were added. Oops! He almost forgot the cookies!

1. What was the first item Kerry put in the paper bag?
   ○ **cookies**
   ○ **sandwiches**
   ○ **water bottle**
   ○ **NH**

2. What was Kerry doing?
   ○ **packing food for a trip**
   ○ **fixing his breakfast**
   ○ **making dinner**
   ○ **NH**

3. Where was Kerry going?
   ○ **to his friend's house**
   ○ **on a picnic**
   ○ **on a bike trip**
   ○ **NH**

4. How many fruits did Kerry put into the bag?
   ○ **4**
   ○ **5**
   ○ **6**
   ○ **NH**

5. Why did Kerry add ice to the bottle of water?
   ○ **to make more water**
   ○ **to cool the water**
   ○ **to keep the food cool**
   ○ **NH**

6. Why did Kerry decide not to take the pickles?
   ○ **he doesn't like pickles**
   ○ **the jar might break**
   ○ **the pickles were too sour**
   ○ **NH**

7. How old is Kerry?
   ○ **10**
   ○ **13**
   ○ **17**
   ○ **NH**

8. Which of these places would Kerry probably <u>not</u> be going?
   ○ **on a picnic**
   ○ **to a restaurant**
   ○ **to the beach**
   ○ **NH**

Name _____

DIRECTIONS:
Read each story, then read each question. Read all the answers, then mark the space for the answer you think is right. Mark NH (not here) if the answer can't be figured out from the given information.

It was the morning of the school spelling bee. Greg's stomach was in knots. Had he studied well enough? Would he look foolish in front of everyone? Greg stood on the stage with the other children. As the teacher went through the group, Greg spelled his words correctly. Soon there were only two students left, Greg and Polly! The teacher asked Polly to spell "nervous." Polly spelled it the wrong way. Greg looked at the teacher and began to grin. He knew he could spell that word!

1. Who is the main character in this story?
   ○ **Greg**
   ○ **Polly**
   ○ **the teacher**
   ○ **NH**

2. Why was Greg's stomach in knots?

   ○ **he had a cold**
   ○ **he didn't want to go to school**
   ○ **he was nervous**
   ○ **NH**

3. What was the name of Polly and Greg's school?
   ○ **Keller Elementary School**
   ○ **Woodlake Middle School**
   ○ **Bradshaw School**
   ○ **NH**

4. How many children were in the spelling bee when it started?

   ○ **a lot**
   ○ **twenty-five**
   ○ **two**
   ○ **NH**

5. What word did Polly misspell?

   ○ **encyclopedia**
   ○ **nervous**
   ○ **a hard word**
   ○ **NH**

6. What word would best describe Greg's feelings at the beginning of the contest?
   ○ **worried**
   ○ **excited**
   ○ **calm**
   ○ **NH**

7. Why did Greg grin at the teacher at the end of the story?
   ○ **Polly had missed the word**
   ○ **Greg knew he could win**
   ○ **He liked the teacher**
   ○ **NH**

8. What had Greg done to prepare for the spelling bee?
   ○ **combed his hair**
   ○ **studied the words**
   ○ **acted foolish for his friends**
   ○ **NH**

Name _____

DIRECTIONS:
Read each story, then read each question. Read all the answers, then mark the space for the answer you think is right. Mark NH (not here) if the answer can't be figured out from the given information.

Beth and Erin wanted to surprise their mother with breakfast in bed. They got up early and raced to the kitchen. Beth measured flour and milk while Erin mixed in the eggs and spices. The girls heated a large flat pan and poured out four perfect pancakes. When the tops were bubbled, Erin carefully flipped them over. Beth fixed a tray with a glass of orange juice and a fork. Erin put the finished pancakes on a plate and slid it onto the tray. Breakfast looked wonderful, but the kitchen was a mess!

1. What are the names of the girls in this story?
   - ○ **Beth and Mother**
   - ○ **Erin and Beth**
   - ○ **Beth and Evan**
   - ○ **NH**

2. What were the girls making for breakfast?
   - ○ **eggs and juice**
   - ○ **eggs and pancakes**
   - ○ **pancakes and juice**
   - ○ **NH**

3. Why were the two girls making breakfast?
   - ○ **to surprise mother**
   - ○ **they were hungry**
   - ○ **for a girl scout badge**
   - ○ **NH**

4. How did they know when to turn the pancake?
   - ○ **the bottom was done**
   - ○ **the top was bubbly**
   - ○ **the pancakes started to smoke**
   - ○ **NH**

5. Why were the girls trying to surprise their mother?
   - ○ **it was her birthday**
   - ○ **it was Mother's Day**
   - ○ **Mother had been working hard**
   - ○ **NH**

6. How many pancakes did the girls make?
   - ○ 2
   - ○ 4
   - ○ 6
   - ○ NH

7. What was on the finished tray?
   - ○ juice, pancakes, fork
   - ○ fork, plate, juice, flower
   - ○ plate, pancakes, juice, fork
   - ○ NH

8. What relationship do the girls share?
   - ○ they are sisters
   - ○ they are cousins
   - ○ they are friends
   - ○ NH

Name _____

DIRECTIONS:
Read each story, then read each question. Read all the answers, then mark the space for the answer you think is right. Mark NH (not here) if the answer can't be figured out from the given information.

Troop 347 was camping. The tents were set up and all the girls were having a lot of fun. Everyone but Elly, that is. Elly was a little worried. She had never stayed out overnight without her parents. She was afraid she might get homesick and cry. All the other girls would laugh and tease her. That night the girls crawled into their sleeping bags and giggled in the dark. Elly didn't know what to do. She was scared. She closed her eyes and thought about her own room with her parents next door. Before she knew it, Elly was asleep!

1. What was the number of Elly's scout troop?
○ **347**
○ **437**
○ **743**
○ **NH**

2. Where were the scouts sleeping?
○ **in cabins**
○ **under the stars**
○ **in tents**
○ **NH**

3. What was Elly's problem?
○ **she hated camping**
○ **she didn't have any friends**
○ **she was homesick**
○ **NH**

4. Which words from the story best tell how Elly is feeling?
○ **camping, tease, parents**
○ **worried, scared, afraid**
○ **dark, overnight, crawled**
○ **NH**

5. How did Elly solve her problem?
○ **she pretended to be home**
○ **she told the troop leader**
○ **she stayed awake all night**
○ **NH**

6. Where did the troop go camping?
○ **in the mountains**
○ **in the forest**
○ **by the ocean**
○ **NH**

7. How did the other girls feel about the camping trip?
○ **they were scared, too**
○ **they wanted to go home**
○ **they were having a good time**
○ **NH**

8. How many girls were in Elly's tent when they went to bed?
○ **four**
○ **seven**
○ **ten**
○ **NH**

Name _____

DIRECTIONS:
Read each story, then read each question. Read all the answers, then mark the space for the answer you think is right. Mark NH (not here) if the answer can't be figured out from the given information.

The city lay spread out beneath the plane as Bob looked out the window of the airplane. The Statue of Liberty stood with her arm raised high in the sky. Bob was very excited. This was his first trip to the city, and there were many things he wanted to do. His family had tickets to a Broadway play for that evening. Bob had read about the city and knew just what he wanted to see. He was going to the Empire State Building because it was one of the tallest skyscrapers. He also wanted to take a carriage ride through Central Park.

1. Who is Bob going to be with while he visits this city?
   - O **his uncle**
   - O **his friend**
   - O **his family**
   - O **NH**

2. What city is Bob coming to visit?
   - O **Chicago**
   - O **New York**
   - O **San Francisco**
   - O **NH**

3. Why is Bob so excited?
   - O **there are so many things to see**
   - O **he has never flown before**
   - O **he is coming to a new country**
   - O **NH**

4. What words in the story help you know which city Bob is going to visit?
   - O **Statue of Liberty, Broadway**
   - O **skyscrapers, carriage**
   - O **plane, city**
   - O **NH**

5. What will Bob go see first when the plane lands?
   - O **Empire State Building**
   - O **Statue of Liberty**
   - O **a Broadway play**
   - O **NH**

6. Where does Bob live?
   - O **Central Park**
   - O **New York**
   - O **San Francisco**
   - O **NH**

7. Where does Bob want to go to ride in a carriage?
   - O **Statue of Liberty**
   - O **Central Park**
   - O **Broadway**
   - O **NH**

8. What word best tells how Bob is feeling as he flies over this city?
   - O **fierce**
   - O **angry**
   - O **cheerful**
   - O **NH**

Name _____

DIRECTIONS:
Read each story, then read each question. Read all the answers, then mark the space for the answer you think is right. Mark NH (not here) if the answer can't be figured out from the given information.

My grandpa is one of the nicest people I know. He lives far away, but I see him many times each year. My Grandpa calls me twice a week, and we talk for a long time! When Grandpa comes to visit, we take walks by the river. We go to the movies and fly kites. Grandpa showed me how to make a model airplane out of toothpicks and tissue paper. He is always ready to play baseball or soccer whenever I want. He is never too busy to listen to me. I think he is the best grandpa anyone ever had!

1. Who is this story about?
   - ○ my father
   - ○ my grandfather
   - ○ me
   - ○ NH

2. How many times does Grandpa visit me each year?
   - ○ twice
   - ○ four times
   - ○ many times
   - ○ NH

3. Where does my grandpa live?
   - ○ far away
   - ○ next door
   - ○ in the next state
   - ○ NH

4. What words do I use in this story to describe my grandpa?
   - ○ baseball and models
   - ○ best and nicest
   - ○ twice and visit
   - ○ NH

5. Who is telling this story?
   - ○ a niece
   - ○ a grandson
   - ○ a granddaughter
   - ○ NH

6. What word best describes my time with Grandpa?
   - ○ unfair
   - ○ dreadful
   - ○ pleasant
   - ○ NH

7. What is something Grandpa would never do with me?
   - ○ go bowling
   - ○ ride bikes
   - ○ play a game
   - ○ NH

8. How do you think Grandpa feels when he comes to visit me?
   - ○ disappointed
   - ○ stubborn
   - ○ merry
   - ○ NH

Name _____

DIRECTIONS:
Read each story, then read each question. Read all the answers, then mark the space for the answer you think is right. Mark NH (not here) if the answer can't be figured out from the given information.

Lucy sat down at the computer and began to write a letter to her pen pal, Jenny. Lucy wrote about the project she was doing in school. Her class had collected a lot of stones and was sorting them by color and shape. They were going to find out about each stone and write reports about them. Lucy knew that Jenny lived near the mountains. She wanted Jenny to find a stone and mail it to her. Lucy was sure that the class would be surprised at the unusual stone she would bring in!

1. Who is Jenny?
   O **Lucy's cousin**
   O **Lucy's pen pal**
   O **Lucy's aunt**
   O **NH**

2. What did Lucy write about in her letter to Jenny?
   O **stones**
   O **the class project**
   O **mountains**
   O **NH**

3. What kind of stone did Lucy want Jenny to send?
   O **a very large stone**
   O **a red stone**
   O **different from what she has**
   O **NH**

4. Why did Lucy want Jenny to send a stone?
   O **to surprise the class**
   O **to look for gold**
   O **to add to Lucy's rock collection**
   O **NH**

5. How did Lucy and Jenny become pen pals?
   O **they looked for stones together**
   O **they met at the beach**
   O **they were good friends**
   O **NH**

6. Where does Jenny live?
   O **near mountains**
   O **near the ocean**
   O **near a big river**
   O **NH**

7. What will the class do with the stones?
   O **display them for the school**
   O **find out what kind they are**
   O **mail them to Jenny**
   O **NH**

8. What word might best describe Lucy's class when they see the unusual stone?
   O **thirsty**
   O **ashamed**
   O **curious**
   O **NH**

Name _____

DIRECTIONS:
Read each story, then read each question. Read all the answers, then mark the space for the answer you think is right. Mark NH (not here) if the answer can't be figured out from the given information.

Dan felt the car begin to shake as if he were driving over rocks. The road looked smooth. He slowed down and pulled over to the edge of the road. Dan got out of the car and walked to the back. The back tire on the passenger side was flat! Dan was already late and didn't need this problem. He opened the trunk and took out the jack. Before long, he was ready to replace the flat tire. Dan looked in the trunk to find the spare tire. As he took it out, he noticed that the spare tire was flat, too! Now what was he going to do?

1. What would be a good name for this story?
   ○ Dan
   ○ How to Change a Flat Tire
   ○ Dan and the Flat Tire
   ○ NH

2. Where was Dan when he got the flat tire?
   ○ in the city
   ○ in the country
   ○ in a park
   ○ NH

3. What did Dan take from the trunk first?
   ○ the spare tire
   ○ a jack
   ○ his jacket
   ○ NH

4. How did Dan know something was wrong with the car?
   ○ he could feel it shaking
   ○ he could hear it banging
   ○ he saw the glass he ran over
   ○ NH

5. Why was Dan unhappy about the flat tire?
   ○ he didn't have a spare
   ○ he was already late
   ○ he wasn't unhappy
   ○ NH

6. How did Dan get a flat tire?
   ○ it was old and just wore out
   ○ he ran over some glass
   ○ he ran over some nails
   ○ NH

7. What word would best describe how Dan is feeling at the end of the story?
   ○ powerful
   ○ hopeless
   ○ content
   ○ NH

8. What would be a good thing for Dan to do now?
   ○ find a phone and get help
   ○ drive on the flat tire
   ○ wait until someone misses him
   ○ NH

Name _____

DIRECTIONS:
Read each story, then read each question. Read all the answers, then mark the space for the answer you think is right. Mark NH (not here) if the answer can't be figured out from the given information.

Mike and Joe were sitting in front of the television. It was Friday and Joe was spending the night at Mike's house. They planned on staying up all night! They watched a movie, then made some popcorn. Joe got out the checkers and the boys played three games. Mike turned out the lights and they made silly shadows on the wall with their flashlights. The boys began to yawn, but they told each other they were not tired. Mike looked at the clock. It was only eleven o'clock. What a long night!

1. In whose house were the boys spending the night?
○ Joe's
○ Mike's
○ Mike and Joe's
○ NH

2. What did the boys do first?

○ watch a movie
○ play checkers
○ eat popcorn
○ NH

3. Why did the boys begin to yawn?
○ they were bored
○ they were tired
○ it was warm in the room
○ NH

4. How many games of checkers did the boys play?
○ two
○ three
○ four
○ NH

5. How old are the boys?
○ eight
○ nine
○ ten
○ NH

6. How did the boys feel at the beginning of the story?
○ terrible
○ excited
○ lonely
○ NH

7. How did the boys feel at the end of the story?
○ wide awake
○ important
○ tired
○ NH

8. What did the boys do after eleven o'clock?
○ watch television
○ eat more popcorn
○ play a game
○ NH

Name _____

DIRECTIONS:
Read each story, then read each question. Read all the answers, then mark the space for the answer you think is right. Mark NH (not here) if the answer can't be figured out from the given information.

Casey's mom was having a garage sale. She had one last year, too, so Casey was not surprised to see her old clothes and toys in the boxes. Many people had come to the house and were looking at the things spread on the driveway. Suddenly Casey saw her favorite bear in one of the boxes. A little boy was just picking it up. He asked his mom if he could have it. Casey wanted to cry. She had not wanted her bear to be in the sale! The boy's mother was handing him some money.

1. What would be a good title for this story?
   ○ **Casey's Bear**
   ○ **The Garage Sale Mistake**
   ○ **A Sale**
   ○ **NH**

2. Who is the main character in this story?
   ○ **the boy**
   ○ **Casey's mom**
   ○ **Casey**
   ○ **NH**

3. How did Casey feel when she saw that the boy wanted her bear?
   ○ **upset**
   ○ **worried**
   ○ **angry**
   ○ **NH**

4. Who put the bear in the garage sale?
   ○ **Casey**
   ○ **Casey's mom**
   ○ **the boy**
   ○ **NH**

5. Why did the mother hand money to the boy?
   ○ **it was his money**
   ○ **she wanted him to hold it**
   ○ **to buy the bear**
   ○ **NH**

6. How did Casey learn about garage sales?
   ○ **they had one last year**
   ○ **she had been to many of them**
   ○ **she read about them**
   ○ **NH**

7. Who came to the garage sale?
   ○ **neighbors**
   ○ **friends**
   ○ **no one**
   ○ **NH**

8. Which sentence best describes how Casey feels about her bear?
   ○ **Casey thinks the bear is smart.**
   ○ **Casey wants to sell the bear.**
   ○ **Casey loves the bear.**
   ○ **NH**

Name _____

DIRECTIONS:
Read each story, then read each question. Read all the answers, then mark the space for the answer you think is right. Mark NH (not here) if the answer can't be figured out from the given information.

My favorite place in the world is the beach. I like to hear the waves as they roar onto the shore. The wind blows a little of the spray in my face if I sit close enough. Sometimes I like to lay in the sand close to the water. The waves lift my legs, and they float a little before the water slips away. There is nothing better than to feel the warm sun on my back and the cool water on my feet! I like to build sand castles, too. Once I made one that was over five feet tall!

1. Who is telling this story?
   - ○ **a boy**
   - ○ **a girl**
   - ○ **an adult**
   - ○ **NH**

2. Where is my favorite place?
   - ○ **in the sand**
   - ○ **in the water**
   - ○ **at the beach**
   - ○ **NH**

3. What does the wind blow into my face?
   - ○ **sand**
   - ○ **water**
   - ○ **sun**
   - ○ **NH**

4. How tall was the castle I once made?
   - ○ **five feet**
   - ○ **six feet**
   - ○ **seven feet**
   - ○ **NH**

5. What is a good title for this story?
   - ○ **Sunny Days**
   - ○ **Building Sand Castles**
   - ○ **My Favorite Place**
   - ○ **NH**

6. What don't I talk about doing at the beach?
   - ○ **cooling my feet**
   - ○ **building castles**
   - ○ **swimming**
   - ○ **NH**

7. Which is my favorite thing to do at the beach?
   - ○ **float on the waves**
   - ○ **build sand castles**
   - ○ **feel the warm sun**
   - ○ **NH**

8. What words might describe how I feel when I am at the beach?
   - ○ **weak**
   - ○ **wonderful**
   - ○ **wealthy**
   - ○ **NH**

DIRECTIONS: Read each story, then read each question.   Read all the answers then mark the space for the answer you think is right. Mark NH (not here) if the answer can't be figured out from the story.

Earth is a large round planet. As it travels around the Sun it rotates, or spins. Let's say it is noon, and the Sun is straight above your head. Earth rotates, turning you away from the Sun. As Earth turns toward the east, the Sun seems to sink lower in the sky. When you can no longer see the Sun, your part of Earth is facing space, and the sky is dark. It is night. Earth keeps rotating until the Sun can be seen in the eastern sky. Before long, the Sun is directly overhead again. This is called a rotation. It takes Earth one day or 24 hours to rotate once.

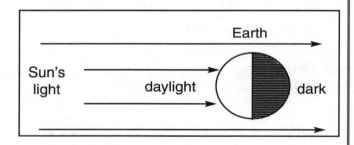

1. What is a good title for this story?
O **The Earth**
O **The Sun**
O **Day and Night**
O **NH**

2. How many hours are in one day?
O **12**
O **18**
O **24**
O **NH**

3. What is another word for "rotate"?
O **Earth**
O **spin**
O **eastern**
O **NH**

4. What causes Earth to become dark?
O **Earth turns west**
O **Earth turns away from the Sun**
O **the Sun goes out**
O **NH**

5. What is it called when Earth goes all the way around the Sun?
O **rotation**
O **space**
O **Earth**
O **NH**

6. When you can't see the Sun, what is Earth facing?
O **other suns**
O **night**
O **space**
O **NH**

7. How long does it take for Earth to rotate once?
O **one week**
O **24 hours**
O **2 days**
O **NH**

Name _____

DIRECTIONS: Read each story, then read each question. Read all the answers then mark the space for the answer you think is right. Mark NH (not here) if the answer can't be figured out from the story.

Earth has a North Pole and a South Pole. A pretend line called the axis goes from the North Pole through Earth to the South Pole. The axis is tilted, or slanted a little to one side. As Earth revolves, or goes around the Sun, at times the North Pole is turned toward the Sun. When this happens, the northern half of Earth gets more sunlight and warms up. We call this "summer." At the same time, the southern half gets less sunlight and has "winter." When Earth goes to the other side of the Sun, the southern half of Earth gets more sunlight. It has summer while the north has winter. The movement around the Sun and the tilted axis are what give Earth its four seasons!

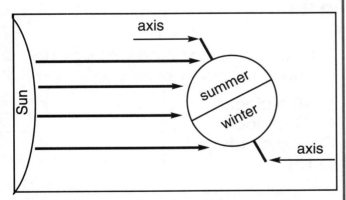

1. What is the name of the imaginary line that runs through Earth?

○ **North Pole**
○ **South Pole**
○ **axis**
○ **NH**

2. Why does each pole get more or less sunlight at different times of the year?

○ **Earth spins around the Sun**
○ **the axis is tilted**
○ **the Sun pulls away from Earth**
○ **NH**

3. What is summer?

○ **when the North Pole gets sunlight**
○ **when half of Earth gets more sunlight than the other half**
○ **when the South Pole gets sunlight**
○ **NH**

4. What causes Earth's seasons?

○ **North Pole and South Pole**
○ **the Sun and the Moon**
○ **tilted axis and revolution**
○ **NH**

5. How many seasons are in a year?

○ **two**
○ **three**
○ **four**
○ **NH**

6. How long is one revolution around the Sun?

○ **one day**
○ **one week**
○ **one month**
○ **NH**

Name _____

DIRECTIONS: Read each story, then read each question. Read all the answers then mark the space for the answer you think is right. Mark NH (not here) if the answer can't be figured out from the story.

Summer is the warm season or time of year. Our part of Earth is tilted toward the Sun. It gets more hours of sunlight which helps warm the land, air, and water. During the summer, people wear light clothing and go swimming to keep cool. They wear hats, lotion, and sunglasses to protect their skin and eyes from the bright light. It is easy to get sunburned if you don't protect your skin! There are more hours of daylight than hours of darkness, so we can stay up later and enjoy the outdoors more.

1. What would be a good title for this story?
   ○ **Keeping Cool**
   ○ **Summer**
   ○ **Wear a Hat!**
   ○ **NH**

2. What is one way to protect your eyes from the bright sunlight?
   ○ **go swimming**
   ○ **wear a hat with a big brim**
   ○ **put lotion on**
   ○ **NH**

3. Which is true of the summer?
   ○ **there are more hours of darkness**
   ○ **there are more hours of sunlight**
   ○ **there are less hours of sunlight**
   ○ **NH**

4. What do most people do during the summer?
   ○ **eat more**
   ○ **drive to the mountains**
   ○ **stay inside**
   ○ **NH**

5. What wouldn't you do to keep yourself cooler in the summer?
   ○ **wear lighter clothes**
   ○ **wear a coat to keep the sunlight off**
   ○ **go swimming**
   ○ **NH**

6. What does the word "season" mean?
   ○ **time of year**
   ○ **summer**
   ○ **protection**
   ○ **NH**

7. How late do most people stay up during the summer season?
   ○ **10 o'clock**
   ○ **11 o'clock**
   ○ **12 o'clock**
   ○ **NH**

8. Why do we get sunburned so easily in the summer?
   ○ **the Earth is tilted toward the Sun**
   ○ **the air is so warm**
   ○ **Earth is tilted away from the Sun**
   ○ **NH**

Name _____

DIRECTIONS: Read each story, then read each question. Read all the answers then mark the space for the answer you think is right. Mark NH (not here) if the answer can't be figured out from the story.

After it rains, the grass is wet, and puddles are on the sidewalk. The warm sunlight and the wind work together to evaporate the water. *Evaporate* means to turn water into a gas called water vapor. The water vapor rises and sticks to small pieces of dust in the air. As the air rises, it gets cooler and the water vapor condenses, or turns back to water. Dust and condensation gather in a group and form a cloud. As the cloud gathers more condensation, it gets darker. Soon the cloud cannot hold all the water. It falls back to Earth as precipitation. Precipitation is any form of water that falls from a cloud to the ground. The process of evaporation, condensation, and precipitation is called the water cycle.

1. What is the main idea of this story?

   ○ **Precipitation is Water**
   ○ **The Water Cycle**
   ○ **Clouds**
   ○ **NH**

2. What does rising water vapor condense on?

   ○ **clouds**
   ○ **pieces of dust**
   ○ **warm air**
   ○ **NH**

3. What does the word "evaporate" mean?

   ○ **disappear**
   ○ **turn into water vapor**
   ○ **turn back into water**
   ○ **NH**

4. How long does it take for water to condense?

   ○ **after a storm**
   ○ **until a cloud forms**
   ○ **three hours of sunlight and wind**
   ○ **NH**

5. Which of these things is not a kind of precipitation?

   ○ **dust particles**
   ○ **sleet**
   ○ **snow**
   ○ **NH**

6. What is it called when water falls, evaporates, forms into clouds, and falls again?

   ○ **condensation**
   ○ **water cycle**
   ○ **precipitation**
   ○ **NH**

7. How does the dust get into the air?

   ○ **from farms**
   ○ **the water cycle leaves it behind**
   ○ **dirt blows into the sky**
   ○ **NH**

Name _____

DIRECTIONS: Read each story, then read each question. Read all the answers then mark the space for the answer you think is right. Mark NH (not here) if the answer can't be figured out from the story.

One of the four seasons is the fall, or autumn. Hours of daylight and dark are about the same during the fall. The weather becomes cooler, and living things get ready for the cold winter months ahead.

The foods we get from many plants are ready to be picked. Many of the summer plants turn brown and die. Their growing season is over. Other plants, like some trees, put their energy into their roots, letting the leaves slowly turn color and fall from the branches.

Animals gather and store nuts and seeds to eat later in the winter. They build nests inside trees or under the ground where they are more protected from the cold. Some animals grow more fur to help keep them warm. Many birds fly south, or migrate, for the winter.

People also use the fall to prepare for winter. Farmers gather their crops and store them in cool, dry places. People make sure their homes are tight so the cold winds won't get in. They take out heavier clothes like coats and sweaters to protect them from the cooler temperatures.

1. What is the main idea of this story?

○ **Fall is a fun season.**
○ **Animals prepare for winter.**
○ **Living things prepare for winter.**
○ **NH**

2. What season comes after autumn?
○ **fall**
○ **summer**
○ **winter**
○ **NH**

3. How do plants prepare for winter?

○ **grow new leaves**
○ **put energy into their roots**
○ **grow hard outer shells**
○ **NH**

4. What is one way animals <u>don't</u> prepare for winter?

○ **build warmer homes**
○ **grow more fur**
○ **raise, gather, and store their food**
○ **NH**

5. What do animals of the ocean do to prepare for winter?

○ **dig holes on the ocean floor**
○ **grow longer fur**
○ **come to the land**
○ **NH**

6. Which way to prepare for winter is <u>not</u> mentioned in this story?

○ **migration**
○ **gathering food**
○ **hibernation**
○ **NH**

Name _____

DIRECTIONS: Read each story, then read each question. Read all the answers then mark the space for the answer you think is right. Mark NH (not here) if the answer can't be figured out from the story.

Autumn is the season when many leaves change color and fall off the branches. Trees that lose their leaves are called deciduous. Do you know why this happens? A tree has many tubes, like veins, reaching from the roots to the leaves. Sap flows through the tubes, carrying water and minerals to the leaves. During the cold winter months, the sap would freeze if it stayed in the tubes. The tree would die with the sap all frozen.

When the weather starts to get cool, the sap goes down to the roots to stay for the winter. Without the water supply, the leaves slowly starve to death. They lose their green color and change to orange, yellow, brown or red. They can no longer hold on to the tree, so they fall to the ground. Maybe that is why so many people call the autumn "fall"!

1. What is the main idea of this story?

○ **Why leaves are green**
○ **How trees lose their leaves**
○ **Autumn is a nice season**
○ **NH**

2. Where does the sap go for the winter?

○ **it migrates south with the birds**
○ **to the leaves**
○ **to the roots**
○ **NH**

3. What causes the leaves to die?

○ **they need food**
○ **they need water and minerals**
○ **they need sunshine**
○ **NH**

4. How long is it before the sap returns to the leaves?

○ **six hours**
○ **twenty-five days**
○ **seven months**
○ **NH**

5. Why does sap stay in the roots all winter?

○ **to kill the leaves**
○ **to keep from freezing**
○ **to feed the roots**
○ **NH**

6. What does the word "deciduous" mean?

○ **a tree that loses its leaves**
○ **sap that stays in the roots**
○ **autumn**
○ **NH**

7. Why might people call autumn "fall"?

○ **many people fall in the autumn**
○ **many leaves fall in the autumn**
○ **it just feels like everything is falling**
○ **NH**

DIRECTIONS: Read each story, then read each question. Read all the answers then mark the space for the answer you think is right. Mark NH (not here) if the answer can't be figured out from the story.

Winter is the coldest season of the year. Your part of Earth gets less sunlight and more darkness. Earth does not have enough sunlight to keep it warm. Many times the precipitation from clouds will freeze and fall as snow. Snow may cover the ground for a few months during the winter!

Plants stop growing and some die during the winter. Other plants and seeds are covered by the snow and must wait for spring to warm them up and make them grow

Animals have a hard time finding food. Many will eat what they stored in the fall. Other animals curl up in a hole or cave and hibernate, or go to sleep for the entire winter! Some birds and insects may migrate to warmer parts of the world.

People do not have to hibernate or migrate. They wear warmer clothes and heat their homes to stay warm. Even the deep snows of winter do not stop people. They ski or ride snowmobiles that race across the top of the snow. Some people even invented a sport called hockey just for the winter.

1. What is the main idea of this story?
   - ○ **What animals do in winter**
   - ○ **The winter season**
   - ○ **Plants and animals**
   - ○ **NH**

2. What causes the cold weather of winter?
   - ○ **snow**
   - ○ **sunlight doesn't warm Earth**
   - ○ **the north wind blows**
   - ○ **NH**

3. What makes winter so hard for most animals?
   - ○ **there isn't enough water**
   - ○ **they can't find enough food**
   - ○ **they sleep too much**
   - ○ **NH**

4. Which living thing is bothered the least by winter?
   - ○ **humans**
   - ○ **plants**
   - ○ **birds**
   - ○ **NH**

5. What sport was made to play in the winter?
   - ○ **baseball**
   - ○ **soccer**
   - ○ **hockey**
   - ○ **NH**

6. What does the word "hibernate" mean?
   - ○ **to fly south for the winter**
   - ○ **dress warmly and face the winter**
   - ○ **to sleep all winter**
   - ○ **NH**

Name _____

DIRECTIONS: Read each story, then read each question. Read all the answers then mark the space for the answer you think is right. Mark NH (not here) if the answer can't be figured out from the story.

During the cold winter months, the sky is often full of gray clouds. The clouds are full of water, just like they are in the summer months. They become full of water and fall to the ground. However, the air between the clouds and the ground is colder at this time of year. The water drops that fall from the clouds freeze as they fall to the ground. These frozen droplets are called snow. Each snowflake is unusual because it freezes in a different pattern as it falls to the ground. The first snows of winter quickly melt when they land. That is because the ground is still a little warm from the summer months. As more snow falls, the ground freezes as well, and the snow will not melt as quickly. The ground will freeze as far as three feet below the grass! The snow will melt, and the ground will thaw as the weather gets warmer.

1. What do we call frozen flakes of water that fall in the winter?

○ rain
○ hail
○ snow
○ NH

2. Why is each snowflake unusual?

○ they have seven points
○ they freeze differently
○ they melt when they land
○ NH

3. What makes the water freeze as it falls?

○ it falls very fast
○ it falls through colder air
○ it freezes before it falls
○ NH

4. Why is the air colder in winter than in summer?

○ we do not get as much sunshine
○ Earth is farther from the Sun
○ it spreads from the South Pole
○ NH

5. How deep will the snow get on the ground?

○ three feet
○ two feet
○ five feet
○ NH

6. What happens when spring comes?

○ snow melts and the ground thaws
○ we get even more snow
○ snow freezes in new patterns
○ NH

7. Which sport would most likely not be done outside in the winter?

○ ice skating
○ water skiing
○ snow skiing
○ NH

Name _____

DIRECTIONS: Read each story, then read each question. Read all the answers then mark the space for the answer you think is right. Mark NH (not here) if the answer can't be figured out from the story.

Spring is the season that comes after winter and before summer. Our part of Earth begins to turn back toward the Sun. We get more hours of sunlight that help warm the air and ground. Snow melts and warmer rain falls. The grass turns green again. Sap returns to the trees, new leaves form, and plants begin to grow. Birds migrate north, and other animals come out of hibernation, or a long winter nap. Earth seems to come alive with new growth. Many animals build new homes and have babies during the spring. This is the season where everything feels fresh and new. People put away their heavy winter clothes and take out umbrellas. Children put away ice skates and sleds. They take out roller skates and bicycles. Spring is here!

1. When does the spring season come?

   ○ **between summer and fall**
   ○ **between winter and summer**
   ○ **between summer and winter**
   ○ **NH**

2. What changes happen to the Earth in spring?

   ○ **the ground and air get colder**
   ○ **the Sun warms the ground and air**
   ○ **rain freezes and the ground thaws**
   ○ **NH**

3. What are the first plants that grow in the spring?

   ○ **flowers**
   ○ **trees**
   ○ **grass**
   ○ **NH**

4. What would be a good title for this story?

   ○ **The Animals Wake Up!**
   ○ **Spring Brings Changes to the Earth**
   ○ **Put Away Your Sleds!**
   ○ **NH**

5. What does the word "hibernation" mean?

   ○ **building new homes**
   ○ **returning to the north**
   ○ **sleeping all winter**
   ○ **NH**

6. What makes Earth warm up in the spring?

   ○ **the wind blows from the south**
   ○ **there are more hours of sunlight**
   ○ **it just happens that way**
   ○ **NH**

7. Why are animals more active in the spring than during the winter?

   ○ **they are too warm**
   ○ **they are not as tired**
   ○ **they are afraid of snow**
   ○ **NH**

Name _____

DIRECTIONS: Read each story, then read each question. Read all the answers then mark the space for the answer you think is right. Mark NH (not here) if the answer can't be figured out from the story.

Plants do not make babies the same way animals do. Plants make seeds that grow into new plants. Some plants make their seeds inside flowers. Roses, tulips, and daisies are some of the flowers that make seeds. Other plants make seeds inside their fruit. Blueberries, apples, and melons all hold the seeds of their plants. Nuts are also the seeds of plants. Pecans, acorns, almonds, and peanuts are all seeds. The pine tree makes its seeds in a cone.

Seeds get to the ground in many ways. Animals may eat fruit and carry the seeds to far off places. Squirrels gather nuts and bury them to eat later. Some of the nuts don't get eaten and may grow into new plants. Birds and bees help to spread the seeds of flowering plants. No matter how they get to the ground, most plants started out as seeds!

1. Which of these is <u>not</u> a seed?

   ○ **peanut**
   ○ **walnut**
   ○ **apple**
   ○ **NH**

2. Which animals help spread the seeds of flowers?
   ○ **bears and rabbits**
   ○ **bees and birds**
   ○ **squirrels and birds**
   ○ **NH**

3. Where does a cactus make its seeds?
   ○ **nuts**
   ○ **cones**
   ○ **leaves**
   ○ **NH**

4. How do animals help make new plants?
   ○ **they plant seedlings**
   ○ **they help spread seeds**
   ○ **they eat the flowers**
   ○ **NH**

5. Which of these plants makes seeds inside flowers?
   ○ **oak trees**
   ○ **apple trees**
   ○ **dandelions**
   ○ **NH**

6. How many types of seeds are named in this story?
   ○ **two**
   ○ **three**
   ○ **four**
   ○ **NH**

7. What would be a good name for this story?
   ○ **The Way Plants Grow**
   ○ **Plants Come From Seeds**
   ○ **Seeds Taste Good**
   ○ **NH**

Name _____

DIRECTIONS: Read each story, then read each question. Read all the answers then mark the space for the answer you think is right. Mark NH (not here) if the answer can't be figured out from the story.

Have you ever looked up into the sky and wondered about clouds? What are they? Where did they come from? Clouds are made when heat makes water evaporate, or become a gas called water vapor. The water vapor rises in the air until it starts to cool. It clings to small pieces of dust in the air and condenses, or turns back into a liquid. These small water droplets and dust gather together and soon form a cloud. Some clouds are thin wisps in the sky. Others are puffy and round, like balls of cotton. Sometimes the puffy ones turn gray or black. These clouds are full of water and cannot hold much more! Clouds help Earth, too. They give us shade on hot summer days. Clouds give us rain that makes things grow. Clouds also give us the snow that makes winter more fun!

1. What two things make a cloud?

   ○ **dust and water**
   ○ **water and cotton**
   ○ **gas and water vapor**
   ○ **NH**

2. What is about to happen when a cloud turns gray or black?

   ○ **it will get warmer**
   ○ **it will get cooler**
   ○ **it will rain or snow**
   ○ **NH**

3. How does heat help make a cloud?

   ○ **heat causes condensation**
   ○ **heat causes rain**
   ○ **heat causes evaporation**
   ○ **NH**

4. What is another name for water that has turned into a gas?

   ○ **condensation**
   ○ **evaporation**
   ○ **water vapor**
   ○ **NH**

5. In which way <u>don't</u> clouds help us?

   ○ **they give us rain**
   ○ **they give us snow**
   ○ **they give us shade**
   ○ **NH**

6. What does "condensation" mean?

   ○ **turning into a gas**
   ○ **turning back into a liquid**
   ○ **turning into water vapor**
   ○ **NH**

7. How big can a cloud get?

   ○ **as big as a country**
   ○ **as big as a mountain**
   ○ **as big as a continent**
   ○ **NH**

Name _____

DIRECTIONS: Read each story, then read each question. Read all the answers then mark the space for the answer you think is right. Mark NH (not here) if the answer can't be figured out from the story.

Every living thing needs water to live. Is rain the only way water comes back to Earth? Not quite. Water can fall from the clouds in a few different ways. During the summer months we usually get rain. Sometimes the air around the clouds is very cold, even in the summer, and the water freezes into balls before it falls. These ice balls are called hail. During the colder months the water passes through cold air and freezes as it falls. These frozen flakes of water are called snow. Sometimes the air is near freezing, and the water falls as both snow and water together! This mixture of snow and water is called sleet. Any water that falls from clouds is called precipitation. Rain, hail, snow, and sleet are four forms of precipitation.

1. What is formed when water in clouds freezes and falls as ice

○ **rain**
○ **hail**
○ **sleet**
○ **NH**

2. What is this story about?

○ **snow**
○ **clouds**
○ **precipitation**
○ **NH**

3. What do we call any water that falls from the clouds?

○ **rain**
○ **ice balls**
○ **precipitation**
○ **NH**

4. What causes snow?

○ **the water freezes before it falls**
○ **the water freezes as it falls**
○ **the water freezes after it falls**
○ **NH**

5. What affects the form of precipitation that will fall?

○ **the air temperature**
○ **the size of the cloud**
○ **the temperature of the ground**
○ **NH**

6. What do we call it when rain, snow, hail, and sleet fall at the same time?

○ **crazy**
○ **snow-rain**
○ **sleet-hail**
○ **NH**

7. What form of precipitation falls to the Earth as liquid water?

○ **snow**
○ **hail**
○ **rain**
○ **NH**

DIRECTIONS:
Read each passage, then read the questions and answers. Decide which is the best answer to the question. Mark the space for the answer you have chosen. Mark the choice NH (not here) if the answer cannot be figured out from the information given.

How to Make Hot Oatmeal

1. Take out all the ingredients you will need: raw oatmeal, brown sugar, a saucepan, a spoon, a measuring cup, water, a bowl.
2. Measure one cup of water and pour it in the saucepan. Put the pan over high heat until it comes to a boil.
3. Measure 2/3 cup of raw oatmeal. Slowly add it to the boiling water, stirring as you pour.
4. Lower the heat and stir the oatmeal, making sure it is mixed totally with the water. Let it warm for six minutes, stirring every two minutes.
5. Remove the oatmeal from the stove. Spoon into a bowl and sprinkle with brown sugar.
6. Add a little milk if you like. Enjoy!

---

1. How many things do you need to make oatmeal?
   - ○ **five**
   - ○ **seven**
   - ○ **nine**
   - ○ **NH**

2. Which of these do you do first?

   - ○ **measure the oatmeal**
   - ○ **stir the oatmeal in the water**
   - ○ **bring the water to a boil**
   - ○ **NH**

3. How much oatmeal do you add to one cup of water?
   - ○ **1/3 cup**
   - ○ **one cup**
   - ○ **2/3 cup**
   - ○ **NH**

4. What fruit tastes best on hot oatmeal?
   - ○ **banana**
   - ○ **apple**
   - ○ **peach**
   - ○ **NH**

5. What ingredient do you sprinkle over the oatmeal?
   - ○ **water**
   - ○ **brown sugar**
   - ○ **cinnamon**
   - ○ **NH**

6. How long should the oatmeal cook before you can eat it?
   - ○ **5 minutes**
   - ○ **6 minutes**
   - ○ **10 minutes**
   - ○ **NH**

Name _____

DIRECTIONS:
Read each passage, then read the questions and answers. Decide which is the best answer to the question. Mark the space for the answer you have chosen. Mark the choice NH (not here) if the answer cannot be figured out from the information given.

Get Ready for School

Before you can walk out the door, you must be ready to go! You can do this first group of things in any order.

- Get dressed (including shoes and socks) and wash your face.
- Eat a good breakfast. Be sure to have some fruit juice as well.
- Get your books and papers ready. Put them in a book bag or backpack to make them easier to carry.

The second group of things can be done in any order, but all of them must be done <u>after</u> the first group.

- Brush your teeth.
- Comb your hair.

This is the last group of things to do before you leave. They must be done in this order.

- Put on a jacket or coat if you need one.
- Open the door and leave.

---

1. Of these three things, which should you do last?

   ○ **get dressed**
   ○ **put on a coat**
   ○ **comb your hair**
   ○ **NH**

2. Which of these should you do first?

   ○ **eat breakfast**
   ○ **pack your books**
   ○ **get dressed**
   ○ **NH**

3. When should you pack your lunch?

   ○ **with the first group**
   ○ **with the second group**
   ○ **with the third group**
   ○ **NH**

4. Which pair can be done in any order?

   ○ **get a coat and pack your books**
   ○ **brush your teeth and get dressed**
   ○ **get dressed and eat breakfast**
   ○ **NH**

5. How many groups have things that can be done in any order?

   ○ **one**
   ○ **two**
   ○ **three**
   ○ **NH**

6. In which group do you brush and comb?

   ○ **Group one**
   ○ **Group two**
   ○ **Group three**
   ○ **NH**

DIRECTIONS:
Read each passage, then read the questions and answers. Decide which is the best answer to the question. Mark the space for the answer you have chosen. Mark the choice NH (not here) if the answer cannot be figured out from the information given.

Flying a Kite

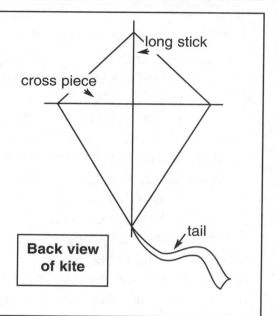

long stick
cross piece
tail

Back view of kite

1. Put together all the things you will need: a kite, a big ball of string, a strip of cloth, two sticks.
2. Put the kite together.
3. Poke or cut a small hole in the kite where the cross piece meets the long stick. Tie one end of your string to the sticks here. Make sure it is tied tightly!
4. Tie the strip of cloth to the bottom of the long stick. This makes a tail to help the kite fly.
5. Go outside and test which way the wind is blowing.
6. Hold the kite facing the wind. Run, let go of the kite, and let out some string!

1. How many things do you need to fly a kite?
   - ○ **two**
   - ○ **three**
   - ○ **five**
   - ○ **NH**

2. Which of these do you do first?
   - ○ **tie the string on the cross piece**
   - ○ **tie on the tail**
   - ○ **put the kite together**
   - ○ **NH**

3. What is the strip of cloth used for?
   - ○ **to hold on to the kite**
   - ○ **to make a tail**
   - ○ **to wipe your hands**
   - ○ **NH**

4. What does the diagram show?
   - ○ **front view**
   - ○ **back view**
   - ○ **side view**
   - ○ **NH**

5. What must be done as soon as you go outside?
   - ○ **hold the kite facing the wind**
   - ○ **let go of the kite**
   - ○ **test the wind's direction**
   - ○ **NH**

6. Which item is not necessary for flying a kite?
   - ○ **ball of string**
   - ○ **heavy piece of wood or stick**
   - ○ **cloth**
   - ○ **NH**

Name _____

DIRECTIONS:
Read each passage, then read the questions and answers. Decide which is the best answer to the question. Mark the space for the answer you have chosen. Mark the choice NH (not here) if the answer cannot be figured out from the information given.

How to Make a Tasty Sandwich

1. Take out all the ingredients you will need: plate, butter knife, tablespoon, jar of peanut butter, jar of jelly, bread (any type).
2. Place two pieces of bread next to each other on the plate.
3. Open the peanut butter. Use the knife to scoop out some peanut butter. Spread it evenly on one slice of bread. Put the lid back on the jar.
4. Open the jelly. Scoop out one tablespoon of jelly and place it on the second piece of bread. Use the knife to spread it evenly on the bread.
5. Pick up the slice of bread with the peanut butter. Place it face down on top of the slice with jelly.
6. Use the knife to cut the sandwich in half.
7. This is even tastier with a glass of cold milk!

---

1. What do these directions help you to make?
   - ○ turkey sandwich
   - ○ jelly sandwich
   - ○ peanut butter and jelly sandwich
   - ○ NH

2. Which of these do you do first?
   - ○ scoop out the jelly
   - ○ put the bread on the plate
   - ○ spread the peanut butter
   - ○ NH

3. What do you use to scoop the peanut butter?
   - ○ a tablespoon
   - ○ a knife
   - ○ a teaspoon
   - ○ NH

4. What happens after you put the bread together?
   - ○ eat the sandwich
   - ○ cut the sandwich
   - ○ spread the jelly
   - ○ NH

5. How old do you have to be to make this kind of sandwich?
   - ○ six years old
   - ○ eight years old
   - ○ nine years old
   - ○ NH

6. How many things do you get together before you begin?
   - ○ 4
   - ○ 5
   - ○ 6
   - ○ NH

DIRECTIONS:
Read each passage, then read the questions and answers. Decide which is the best answer to the question. Mark the space for the answer you have chosen. Mark the choice NH (not here) if the answer cannot be figured out from the information given.

SWIMMING RULES
1. Pool opens at 8:30 a.m. (Monday through Saturday)
2. No diving at any time
3. Running near the pool is not allowed.
4. No eating or drinking in or near the pool
5. A lifeguard must be on duty at all swimming times. If one is not available, you may not use the pool.
6. Please shower before and after use of the pool.
7. No pushing, pulling, or unecessary splashing
8. No rafts, floats, or pool sticks allowed
9. If you are warned about breaking any of these rules, the lifeguard may ask you to leave.
10. Pool closes at 7:00 p.m. (Monday through Saturday)

---

1. How many pool rules are listed on the chart?
   - ○ **ten**
   - ○ **twelve**
   - ○ **twenty**
   - ○ **NH**

2. What time does the pool close?
   - ○ **7:00 a.m.**
   - ○ **8:30 a.m.**
   - ○ **7:00 p.m.**
   - ○ **NH**

3. What does rule number four tell you?
   - ○ **no running**
   - ○ **no eating**
   - ○ **no splashing**
   - ○ **NH**

4. What should you do if a lifeguard is not on duty?
   - ○ **swim carefully**
   - ○ **stay out of the pool**
   - ○ **use a float or raft**
   - ○ **NH**

5. When might the lifeguard ask you to leave?
   - ○ **when you break a rule**
   - ○ **if you don't have a swimcap**
   - ○ **when he wants to have lunch**
   - ○ **NH**

6. What time does the pool open on special holidays?
   - ○ **7:00 a.m.**
   - ○ **8:30 a.m.**
   - ○ **noon**
   - ○ **NH**

Name _____

DIRECTIONS:
Read each passage, then read the questions and answers. Decide which is the best answer to the question. Mark the space for the answer you have chosen. Mark the choice NH (not here) if the answer cannot be figured out from the information given.

How to Make a Clay Elephant
Materials needed: cardboard, modeling clay, scissors, toothpick

Body: Roll a piece of clay into an egg shaped ball. Use a piece of clay about the size of a ping-pong ball.

Head: Roll a piece of clay about the size of a marble into a round ball. Stick it to the body.

Legs: Make a clay "snake" about as wide as your thumb and twice as long as your hand. Cut the "snake" into four equal parts. Stick these legs on the body.

Trunk and tail: Make two smaller "snakes." One should be about the size of your little finger. Stick it on the head for the trunk. The other should be tiny. Stick it on the back of the body for the tail.

Ears: Make two small marbles of clay and flatten them. Stick them on the sides of the head to make ears.

Tusks: Cut two tusks from cardboard and push them into the clay on either side of the trunk.

Eyes: Use the toothpick to poke two little holes in the elephant's head for eyes.

---

1. How many materials do you need to make a clay elephant?

- ○ **three**
- ○ **four**
- ○ **five**
- ○ **NH**

2. Which of these do you make first?

- ○ **tail**
- ○ **ears**
- ○ **head**
- ○ **NH**

3. Which part of the elephant is made last?

- ○ **ears**
- ○ **eyes**
- ○ **tail**
- ○ **NH**

4. How much clay should you use for the elephant's body?

- ○ **the size of a marble**
- ○ **the size of a ping-pong ball**
- ○ **the size of a tennis ball**
- ○ **NH**

5. What part of the elephant is about as wide as your thumb?

- ○ **trunk**
- ○ **tail**
- ○ **legs**
- ○ **NH**

6. How many elephants can you make from one box of clay?

- ○ **3**
- ○ **10**
- ○ **17**
- ○ **NH**

Name _____

DIRECTIONS:
Read each passage, then read the questions and answers. Decide which is the best answer to the question. Mark the space for the answer you have chosen. Mark the choice NH (not here) if the answer cannot be figured out from the information given.

Make String Art!
Cover your work area with newspaper and wear an old shirt!

Materials needed: 4 plastic bowls or cups, paper, 4 spoons, string, 4 colors of paint

1. Use a spoon to scoop some paint into a bowl. Use a different spoon and bowl for each color.
2. Cut four one-foot pieces of string. Hold one piece by the end and dip it into a color. Coat the string with paint. Use the other stings for the other colors.
3. Drop the paint covered string onto the piece of paper. Lift the string and drop it 2 or 3 time to make different patterns. Try wiggling the string to smear the paint.
4. Repeat step three using the other paint colors.
5. Set the painting aside to dry.
6. Use the paintings to decorate your room or make them into greeting cards.

---

1. How many bowls do you need to make string art?
   - ○ **four**
   - ○ **five**
   - ○ **six**
   - ○ **NH**

2. Which of these do you do first?

   - ○ **cut the string**
   - ○ **cover the table with newspaper**
   - ○ **spoon out the paint**
   - ○ **NH**

3. About how long should you cut the pieces of string?
   - ○ **eight inches**
   - ○ **twelve inches**
   - ○ **sixteen inches**
   - ○ **NH**

4. Which colors of paint do you need to make string art?
   - ○ **red, blue, green, yellow**
   - ○ **purple, pink, orange, blue**
   - ○ **black, brown, green, yellow**
   - ○ **NH**

5. How does the paint get from the bowl to the paper?
   - ○ **pour it out**
   - ○ **use a paintbush**
   - ○ **dip string in paint and put on**
   - ○ **NH**

6. What is one suggested use for the finished art?
   - ○ **gift wrap**
   - ○ **book covers**
   - ○ **cards**
   - ○ **NH**

DIRECTIONS:
Read each passage, then read the questions and answers. Decide which is the best answer to the question. Mark the space for the answer you have chosen. Mark the choice NH (not here) if the answer cannot be figured out from the information given.

Easy to Make Gift Ideas

Soft Drink Can Banks: Rinse the can and let it dry. Use paint, felt, yarn, or paper to cover the outside of the can. Glue on buttons, ribbons, feathers or other trimmings. The can opening becomes the money slot.

Treasure Boxes: Use cloth, felt, or paper to cover a shoe box and its lid. Decorate the box by gluing on ornaments, patches, stamps, or whatever you like.

Pebble Pets: Choose ten or twelve pebbles or small rocks that have an unusual color or shape. Wash and dry them. Glue them together to create an animal, person or creature. Paint faces, fangs, scales, feathers, eyes, ears, or whatever you like on you "pets."

---

1. Which material is used in all three gift ideas?
   - O **paint**
   - O **feathers**
   - O **glue**
   - O **NH**

2. On which gift should you paint a face?
   - O **Soft Drink Banks**
   - O **Treasure Boxes**
   - O **Pebble Pets**
   - O **NH**

3. Which gift <u>does not</u> need to be washed before you make it?
   - O **Soft Drink Banks**
   - O **Treasure Boxes**
   - O **Pebble Pets**
   - O **NH**

4. Which gift is made of metal?
   - O **Soft Drink Banks**
   - O **Treasure Boxes**
   - O **Pebble Pets**
   - O **NH**

5. Which gift costs the most to make?
   - O **Soft Drink Banks**
   - O **Treasure Boxes**
   - O **Pebble Pets**
   - O **NH**

6. Which gift is not used to hold something?
   - O **Soft Drink Banks**
   - O **Treasure Boxes**
   - O **Pebble Pets**
   - O **NH**

DIRECTIONS:
Read each passage, then read the questions and answers. Decide which is the best answer to the question. Mark the space for the answer you have chosen. Mark the choice NH (not here) if the answer cannot be figured out from the information given.

Grow a Tree

Growing your own apple tree from a seed can be fun. It just takes a lot of time to grow! **First:** Eat an apple. Be careful to save six or eight of the seeds. **Second:** Rinse the seeds in cool water. **Third:** Wrap the seeds in a paper towel or napkin and put them in a safe place in the refrigerator for about three weeks. **Fourth:** Put the seeds in a cup or glass. Cover them with water. Leave them in a warm place to soak for three or four days. **Fifth**: Plant the seeds in a small pot of soil. Keep them well watered. **Sixth:** When the seedlings grow to be three inches tall, separate them. Give each seed its own pot. **Seventh:** When the apple plants outgrow the pot, plant them in a special place in your yard.
Last: Be patient! It takes a long time to grow into a good sized tree.

---

1. What do you do to the seeds in step four?

   ○ **plant them**
   ○ **rinse them**
   ○ **soak them**
   ○ **NH**

2. Which of these steps should be done first?

   ○ **wrap the seeds in a napkin**
   ○ **chill them in the refrigerator**
   ○ **eat an apple**
   ○ **NH**

3. How many years does it take to grow a full sized apple tree?

   ○ **six**
   ○ **twelve**
   ○ **twenty-five**
   ○ **NH**

4. In which step do you plant the seeds?

   ○ **second**
   ○ **fifth**
   ○ **last**
   ○ **NH**

5. What do you do in the eighth step?

   ○ **put it in a larger pot**
   ○ **plant the tree in the yard**
   ○ **wait**
   ○ **NH**

6. In which step do you separate the seedlings?

   ○ **fifth**
   ○ **sixth**
   ○ **seventh**
   ○ **NH**

Name _____

DIRECTIONS:
Read each letter, then read each question about the letter. Decide which is the best answer to the question. Mark the space for the answer you have chosen. Mark the choice NH (not here) if the answer cannot be figured out from the information given.

September 12, 1999

Hi Keshia,

The most exciting thing happened to me today! Grandma took me to the mall to shop for some new clothes for school. She let me pick out the shoes and pants I wanted. I let her pick out some skirts and a dress, but I liked them so it was alright. Grandma took me to SuperDuper Cuts and I got a really cute new haircut. Grandma and I agree that it looks very nice on me. After that we went to the food court for lunch. A lady kept looking at me and I was getting a little worried so I told my grandma. The lady came over and said she was a casting director for television. She thinks I should try out for a part in a new movie they are going to film! I will tell you all about it in my next letter.

Your friend,
Serina

---

1. Which person wrote this letter?

   ○ **Grandma**
   ○ **Serina**
   ○ **Keshia**
   ○ **NH**

2. Which phrase is the greeting of this letter?

   ○ **September 12**
   ○ **Dear Keshia**
   ○ **Yours Truly**
   ○ **NH**

3. What clothes did Serina buy at the mall?

   ○ **socks, skirts, a dress**
   ○ **shirts, sweaters, a dress**
   ○ **pants, skirts, a dress**
   ○ **NH**

4. Which word best tells how Serina felt when the lady was staring at her?

   ○ **anxious**
   ○ **curious**
   ○ **frightened**
   ○ **NH**

5. Why was the lady looking at Serina?

   ○ **she wants to put Serina in a movie**
   ○ **she wants Serina to sing on T.V.**
   ○ **she thought she knew Serina**
   ○ **NH**

6. Why did Serina look so nice on the day she went shopping?

   ○ **she had on her new clothes**
   ○ **she put on special sunglasses**
   ○ **she got her hair cut a new way**
   ○ **NH**

DIRECTIONS:
Read each letter, then read each question about the letter. Decide which is the best answer to the question. Mark the space for the answer you have chosen. Mark the choice NH (not here) if the answer cannot be figured out from the information given.

October 18, 1999

Dear Brandon,

I am sorry you broke your arm and have to stay home for a week. This morning the teacher told the class all about your accident and said that we should write a letter to you. I broke my leg when I was eight. I fell off the slide at school and landed the wrong way on my leg. I know how you feel about having that cast on. It is heavy and it itches a lot where you can't scratch it. However, it can be kind of fun at times. You will probably get less homework because you can't write with your hand now, and that is really neat! Everybody here at school can hardly wait to write their name on your cast. Besides, all the girls are already thinking up ways to help you when you get back! Rest up, feel better, and we miss you.

Your pal,
Brian

---

1. Who has a broken arm?

O **Brandon**
O **Brian**
O **the teacher**
O **NH**

2. Why did Brian write to Brandon?

O **they are friends**
O **he wanted Brandon to feel better**
O **the teacher told the class to write**
O **NH**

3. What is not one of the neat things about having to wear a cast?

O **kids want to sign it**
O **it itches a lot**
O **everyone wants to be helpful**
O **NH**

4. How did Brian break his leg?

O **in a car accident**
O **jumping from the swings**
O **falling off the slide**
O **NH**

5. How did Brandon break his arm?

O **in a car accident**
O **jumping from the swings**
O **falling off the slide**
O **NH**

6. How long will Brandon be home from school?

O **two days**
O **seven days**
O **fourteen days**
O **NH**

Name _____

DIRECTIONS:
Read each letter, then read each question about the letter. Decide which is the best answer to the question. Mark the space for the answer you have chosen. Mark the choice NH (not here) if the answer cannot be figured out from the information given.

December 27, 1999

Dear Aunt Minka,

I know you could not get home for the holidays this year, but we all thought about you a lot. Momma said her plum pudding is not nearly as good as yours is. Poppa and Vinny often kept looking at the piano and sighing. It just wasn't the same without you playing our favorite songs while we sang along. Baby Kristie learned to say your name and she was looking for you, too. Even the cat seemed to be a little sad because you weren't here. I want you to know that I missed you just as much as they did, but I wasn't so sad about it. I took out all the letters you sent to me this year, and I read each one of them. It made me feel closer to you when I was reading your words. We will see you soon.

Your loving niece,
Denise

---

1. Why was Denise's family a little sad this holiday?

○ **Momma made bad pudding**
○ **Baby Kristie was not well**
○ **Minka did not come home**
○ **NH**

2. Who wanted Minka to play the piano for them?

○ **Kristie and Denise**
○ **Momma and Poppa**
○ **Vinny and Poppa**
○ **NH**

3. Where is Aunt Minka?

○ **traveling the world**
○ **visiting friends**
○ **with her daughter**
○ **NH**

4. How do you know that Aunt Minka is a favorite person in this family?

○ **Momma missed her pudding**
○ **even the cat missed her**
○ **Denise read her letters**
○ **NH**

5. How did Denise make herself feel closer to Aunt Minka?

○ **she reread all of Minka's letters**
○ **she sat in Minka's favorite chair**
○ **she wrote a letter to Minka**
○ **NH**

6. When will Aunt Minka come home?

○ **soon**
○ **next year**
○ **in two months**
○ **NH**

Name _____

DIRECTIONS:
Read each letter, then read each question about the letter. Decide which is the best answer to the question. Mark the space for the answer you have chosen. Mark the choice NH (not here) if the answer cannot be figured out from the information given.

February 14, 2000

Dear Grandpa,

Roses are red and violets are blue,
I can't think of anyone nicer than you.
I looked for a card, but nothing was right.
None of them said the things that I might.
I wanted to ask you in some special way,
Would you please be <u>my</u> valentine today?

Happy Valentine's Day!

Your valentine,
Jessica

---

1. Who wrote this letter?

   ○ **Grandpa**
   ○ **Jessica**
   ○ **Jessica's friend**
   ○ **NH**

2. What do the first two lines tell Grandpa?

   ○ **happy Valentine's Day**
   ○ **Jessica didn't buy a card**
   ○ **Grandpa is a nice person**
   ○ **NH**

3. What is unusual about this letter?

   ○ **Jessica wrote it**
   ○ **it is for Grandpa**
   ○ **it is a poem**
   ○ **NH**

4. Where does Grandpa live?

   ○ **Valentine Lane**
   ○ **Valentine Street**
   ○ **Violet Avenue**
   ○ **NH**

5. Why didn't Jessica just buy a card for Grandpa?

   ○ **none of them said the right things**
   ○ **she couldn't find a pretty one**
   ○ **Jessica didn't have the money**
   ○ **NH**

6. What does Jessica ask Grandpa to do?

   ○ **come to her house**
   ○ **be Jessica's valentine**
   ○ **come to a valentine party**
   ○ **NH**

DIRECTIONS:
Read each letter, then read each question about the letter. Decide which is the best answer to the question. Mark the space for the answer you have chosen. Mark the choice NH (not here) if the answer cannot be figured out from the information given.

March 21, 2000

Hello Graham,

　　　I moved into my new house today. It is bigger than our other house. I even have a room of my very own! Mom said I can have bunk beds to put in my room and I can paint it any color I want. Do you think I should paint it brown like your room or gray like my old room? I stayed outside while the movers put the furniture in the house. A boy name Jake from down the street came over and asked me to go bike riding. He loaned me his old bike because mine wasn't unpacked yet. Jake showed me around the neighborhood and I met a few more kids. I ate dinner at Jake's house. He's a pretty neat guy. Don't worry, though. You are still my very best friend!

　　　　　　　　　　　　　　　Yours truly,
　　　　　　　　　　　　　　　Phillip

---

1. What just happened to Phillip's family?
   - ○ **they ate dinner**
   - ○ **they moved to a new house**
   - ○ **they painted a room**
   - ○ **NH**

2. Why does Phillip like the new house so much?
   - ○ **he has his own room**
   - ○ **it has a pool**
   - ○ **it is in a nice neighborhood**
   - ○ **NH**

3. What color is Graham's bedroom painted?
   - ○ **white**
   - ○ **gray**
   - ○ **brown**
   - ○ **NH**

4. Who is Jake?
   - ○ **Phillip's best friend**
   - ○ **Phillip's new neighbor**
   - ○ **Graham's new friend**
   - ○ **NH**

5. What color was the bike Jake loaned to Phillip?
   - ○ **white**
   - ○ **gray**
   - ○ **brown**
   - ○ **NH**

6. What words from the letter tell you that Phillip misses Graham?
   - ○ **"I can have bunk beds"**
   - ○ **"he's a pretty neat guy"**
   - ○ **"you are still my very best friend"**
   - ○ **NH**

DIRECTIONS:
Read each letter, then read each question about the letter. Decide which is the best answer to the question. Mark the space for the answer you have chosen. Mark the choice NH (not here) if the answer cannot be figured out from the information given.

May 5, 2000

Dear Miss Whitney,

It has been a long year, but it is almost over now! Before summer vacation comes, I would like to tell you how I feel about being in your class this year. Last fall when school started, I wanted to be in Mrs. Sharp's class. You gave us homework on the very first day of school and you haven't miss one day since! You made me work hard and you never would take a paper that wasn't done the right way. I'll never forget that report I had to write seven times before you would let me turn it in! I thought I was unlucky to have you for a teacher, but do you know what? I learned a lot from you. I also had a lot of fun and I like you more than any teacher I've ever had. Thank you for giving me the best year I've ever had!

Your student,
Ken

---

1. Which person will get this letter?

○ **Miss Whitney**
○ **Mrs. Sharp**
○ **Ken**
○ **NH**

2. Who is Mrs. Sharp?

○ **Ken's teacher this year**
○ **the teacher Ken wanted**
○ **Ken wrote to**
○ **NH**

3. What is the purpose of this letter?

○ **to say "I will miss you"**
○ **to say "You were mean"**
○ **to say "Thank you"**
○ **NH**

4. Which word tells how Ken felt about getting this teacher last fall?

○ **wealthy**
○ **unlucky**
○ **pleasant**
○ **NH**

5. Which word tells how Ken feels toward his teacher now?

○ **frightened**
○ **nervous**
○ **thankful**
○ **NH**

6. What grade does Miss Whitney teach?

○ **first grade**
○ **second grade**
○ **third grade**
○ **NH**

DIRECTIONS:
Read each letter, then read each question about the letter. Decide which is the best answer to the question. Mark the space for the answer you have chosen. Mark the choice NH (not here) if the answer cannot be figured out from the information given.

August 6, 2000

Dear Emily,

My parents wanted me to get to know the "Great Outdoors," so they took me camping this summer. We camped right out in the national forest near a lake, not in a campground. We had to fill our buckets with water at a gas station then drive back to camp. There was never enough to waste, so I learned how to use the same water at least three times before throwing it out! At night the only light we had was from the campfire, the stars, and the Moon. It was really dark out there, but I must admit that it was awfully pretty too. There were a few wild animals that came through our camp. I got one chipmunk to eat right out of my hand. I also saw raccoon, deer, opossum, a hawk, and a skunk (phew!!!). I am glad we went camping, but I am also glad to be home.

Yours truly,
Meghan

---

1. Whose family went camping during their summer vacation?

  ○ **Emily's**
  ○ **Meghan's**
  ○ **Susan's**
  ○ **NH**

2. How did the family get the water they needed?

  ○ **from the river**
  ○ **from a lake**
  ○ **from a gas station**
  ○ **NH**

3. Why did it seem so dark at night?

  ○ **there was no campfire**
  ○ **there weren't house or street lights**
  ○ **father would not turn on lights**
  ○ **NH**

4. What animal <u>didn't</u> Meghan see during her camping trip?

  ○ **rabbit**
  ○ **chipmunk**
  ○ **hawk**
  ○ **NH**

5. Which words best describe Meghan's camping trip?

  ○ **nature and far away**
  ○ **comfort and cozy**
  ○ **harbor and friendship**
  ○ **NH**

6. Where will Emily's family take their vacation next year?

  ○ **Disney World**
  ○ **in Colorado**
  ○ **at the beach**
  ○ **NH**

Answer Key

Name _____ Skill: Word Study—Test 1

DIRECTIONS:
One or more letters are underlined in each of the words below. Read each word, then mark the space for the word that has the same sound as the underlined letter or letters.

1. answer — plant ●, late ○, lazy ○
2. study — ribbon ○, blame ○, different ●
3. photograph — grace ●, gurgle ○, scarf ○
4. steam — insect ○, muscle ●, teen ○
5. force — ordinary ●, robin ○, wrote ○
6. oversleep — slant ●, salt ○, clean ○
7. November — fault ○, punish ○, veil ●
8. blame — bullet ○, problem ●, ball ○
9. happen — meet ○, zebra ○, often ●
10. pilot — icy ●, begin ○, silver ○
11. tomorrow — somehow ○, crown ○, groan ●
12. equipment — punish ○, quarter ●, kingdom ○
13. thumb — what ○, both ●, trace ○
14. apply — hind ●, uneasy ○, noisy ○

© Carson-Dellosa CD-3735   1

Name _____ Skill: Word Study—Test 2

DIRECTIONS:
One or more letters are underlined in each of the words below. Read each word, then mark the space for the word that has the same sound as the underlined letter or letters.

1. another — operate ●, each ○, ears ○
2. object — goal ○, giant ●, grab ○
3. crazy — about ○, mail ●, hand ○
4. children — dirt ○, chart ○, dream ●
5. cough — famous ●, ghastly ○, daughter ○
6. noisy — harm ○, handle ●, moist ○
7. understood — balloon ○, crook ●, shampoo ○
8. tomato — unfold ●, perform ○, proof ○
9. choice — echo ○, canoe ○, enjoy ●
10. library — bird ○, broken ●, rib ○
11. before — sweet ○, better ○, care ●
12. describe — isn't ●, until ○, quiet ○
13. plow — powder ●, own ○, blow ○
14. fireplace — rare ●, sneeze ○, swell ○

© Carson-Dellosa CD-3735   2

Name _____ Skill: Word Study—Test 3

DIRECTIONS:
One or more letters are underlined in each of the words below. Read each word, then mark the space for the word that has the same sound as the underlined letter or letters.

1. smash — sample ○, blacksmith ○, shame ●
2. forward — reply ○, velvet ○, waist ●
3. bought — hire ○, bright ●, gather ○
4. bleed — tumbler ●, label ○, bald ○
5. bounce — drove ○, should ○, count ●
6. suggest — jail ○, giggle ●, gentle ○
7. again — ahead ●, day ○, lady ○
8. wealth — thirty ●, shelf ○, hoot ○
9. freeze — mushroom ○, moccasin ○, easy ●
10. streak — parent ○, prize ○, remain ●
11. too — toot ●, so ○, wool ○
12. hurtle — Thursday ●, park ○, rust ○
13. charge — trade ○, hear ○, army ●
14. cent — crest ○, since ●, cart ○

© Carson-Dellosa CD-3735   3

Name _____ Skill: Word Study—Test 4

DIRECTIONS:
One or more letters are underlined in each of the words below. Read each word, then mark the space for the word that has the same sound as the underlined letter or letters.

1. become — circus ○, king ●, cell ○
2. awful — photo ●, clear ○, punish ○
3. thirteen — riddle ○, timid ○, circus ●
4. royal — moist ●, aloud ○, money ○
5. purpose — please ○, walrus ●, crazy ○
6. distrust — turkey ○, tore ○, traffic ●
7. hazy — above ○, April ●, animal ○
8. dentist — greed ○, deal ○, fetch ●
9. delight — ghost ○, false ○, sigh ●
10. lung — naughty ○, length ●, grand ○
11. kangaroo — flute ●, furry ○, bookcase ○
12. snuggle — snatch ○, sunflower ●, singer ○
13. awhile — wrench ○, saw ○, wheat ●
14. odd — golden ○, open ○, mop ●

© Carson-Dellosa CD-3735   4

Answer Key

Top Left — Skill: Word Study—Test 5

Name _____

DIRECTIONS:
One or more letters are underlined in each of the words below. Read each word, then mark the space for the word that has the same sound as the underlined letter or letters.

1. t**o**wer
   - tow ○
   - snow ○
   - hour ●

8. sh**oo**k
   - igloo ○
   - afoot ●
   - broom ○

2. thr**ow**n
   - comfort ○
   - famous ○
   - dinosaur ●

9. l**oo**p
   - cookie ○
   - tooth ●
   - football ○

3. th**ou**sand
   - tough ●
   - though ○
   - ourselves ○

10. **a**ll
   - above ○
   - yawn ●
   - fast ○

4. f**e**male
   - empty ○
   - equal ●
   - ever ○

11. fl**a**vor
   - firm ○
   - film ○
   - afloat ●

5. be**ha**ve
   - photo ○
   - hamburger ●
   - furniture ○

12. ob**j**ect
   - danger ●
   - glue ○
   - grain ○

6. f**o**llow
   - November ○
   - okay ○
   - olive ●

13. sec**o**nd
   - photo ○
   - mother ●
   - explode ○

7. h**ea**p
   - punish ●
   - graph ○
   - afraid ○

14. pre**s**ent
   - juice ○
   - frost ○
   - musical ●

Top Right — Skill: Word Study Skills

Name _____

DIRECTIONS:
Each given word has some underlined letters. Mark the space for the word that has the same sound as the letter or letters that are underlined.

1. in**sp**ect
   - separate ○
   - sip ○
   - spook ●

8. be**t**ween
   - twinkle ●
   - tower ○
   - thrown ○

2. **wr**inkle
   - wore ○
   - worn ○
   - rewrite ●

9. comm**a**
   - space ○
   - away ●
   - label ○

3. sp**a**re
   - jaw ○
   - cause ○
   - careful ●

10. pit**ch**er
   - charm ●
   - cream ○
   - cast ○

4. de**gr**ee
   - deaf ○
   - least ●
   - meadow ○

11. a**fr**aid
   - friend ●
   - refuse ○
   - farewell ○

5. sl**i**t
   - fry ○
   - inch ●
   - jail ○

12. mar**k**et
   - fancy ○
   - face ○
   - picture ●

6. **o**vernight
   - hopeful ●
   - pilot ○
   - odd ○

13. **j**oin
   - crow ○
   - newsboy ●
   - hour ○

7. al**ph**abet
   - great ○
   - pooh ○
   - careful ●

14. de**s**cribe
   - secret ○
   - slice ○
   - scout ●

Bottom Left — Skill: Word Study Skills

Name _____

DIRECTIONS:
Each given word has some underlined letters. Mark the space for the word that has the same sound as the letter or letters that are underlined.

1. thir**st**
   - visitor ○
   - pleasant ○
   - pasture ●

8. **u**nfold
   - flute ○
   - munch ●
   - gurgle ○

2. rela**x**
   - skin ○
   - mixture ●
   - square ○

9. c**au**se
   - caught ●
   - although ○
   - blow ○

3. c**ar**d
   - March ●
   - author ○
   - bare ○

10. **c**limb
   - coal ○
   - call ○
   - click ●

4. p**ea**ch
   - ahead ○
   - feather ○
   - week ●

11. wi**ggle**
   - neighbor ○
   - gentle ○
   - gang ●

5. t**i**de
   - mill ○
   - slice ●
   - laid ○

12. **kn**elt
   - keeper ○
   - kettle ○
   - unlike ●

6. zer**o**
   - obey ●
   - onion ○
   - nor ○

13. c**ou**nt
   - outside ●
   - noble ○
   - object ○

7. **pl**astic
   - flop ○
   - explore ●
   - flipper ○

14. su**nsh**ine
   - shelf ●
   - school ○
   - scrap ○

Bottom Right — Skill: Word Study—Test 8

Name _____

DIRECTIONS:
One or more letters are underlined in each of the words below. Read each word, then mark the space for the word that has the same sound as the underlined letter or letters.

1. **sw**eater
   - tower ○
   - swoop ●
   - twist ○

8. f**u**ture
   - umbrella ○
   - January ●
   - sudden ○

2. **y**awn
   - beyond ●
   - scurry ○
   - heavy ○

9. dr**i**ft
   - excite ○
   - attic ●
   - ice cream ○

3. num**b**er
   - grab ●
   - color ○
   - did ○

10. br**ea**d
   - meat ○
   - beat ○
   - ahead ●

4. se**c**ret
   - race ○
   - crayon ●
   - carol ○

11. **gl**itter
   - hourglass ●
   - lung ○
   - dull ○

5. cr**oa**k
   - motor ●
   - ribbon ○
   - gown ○

12. c**o**ffee
   - broil ○
   - round ○
   - along ●

6. su**r**prise
   - reply ○
   - present ●
   - perch ○

13. **sk**eleton
   - snack ○
   - peck ○
   - basketball ●

7. repor**t**
   - tomorrow ●
   - gather ○
   - thank ○

14. b**u**shy
   - figure ○
   - duty ○
   - pudding ●

Answer Key

Name _____

DIRECTIONS:
One or more letters are underlined in each of the words below. Read each word, then mark the space for the word that has the same sound as the underlined letter or letters.

1. belly				8. kni**fe**		
myself ○	depend ○	money ●		drip ○	continue ○	hire ●

2. t**y**pe				9. villa**g**er		
grand ○	maid ○	lighthouse ●		graham ○	fingertip ●	range ○

3. warm**th**				10. **g**rin		
tongue ○	tank ○	thick ●		gruff ●	guard ○	girl ○

4. f**l**ame				11. mi**st**		
half ○	floppy ●	perform ○		sixth ○	scarf ○	stamp ●

5. chu**ck**le				12. frank		
collection ●	center ○	side ○		squirrel ○	coach ○	dune ●

6. **a**che				13. a**i**m		
fancy ○	escape ●	farewell ○		famous ●	chair ○	nickel ○

7. disturb				14. f**au**lt		
turn ●	rust ○	rub ○		owe ○	water ●	sauce ○

Name _____

DIRECTIONS:
In each question the same word is divided into syllables in three different ways. Decide which is the correct way to divide the word and mark the answer.

1. ● a•board ○ ab•oard ○ abo•ard	7. ○ e•yelash ● eye•lash ○ eyel•ash	13. ○ n•arrow ○ na•rrow ● nar•row
2. ○ a•ccount ● ac•count ○ accou•nt	8. ○ mi•llion ● mil•lion ○ milli•on	14. ○ foo•tprint ● foot•print ○ footpr•int
3. ○ bi•rdhouse ● bird•house ○ birdho•use	9. ○ h•obby ○ ho•bby ● hob•by	15. ○ spid•er ○ sp•ider ● spi•der
4. ● de•pend ○ dep•end ○ depe•nd	10. ● mo•ment ○ mom•ent ○ mome•nt	16. ○ pl•anet ○ pla•net ● plan•et
5. ○ ba•ckward ● back•ward ○ backw•ard	11. ○ mu•mble ● mum•ble ○ mumb•le	17. ● pro•gram ○ prog•ram ○ progr•am
6. ○ chi•pmunk ○ chipm•unk ● chip•munk	12. ○ li•mit ● lim•it ○ limi•t	18. ○ stu•bborn ● stub•born ○ stubb•orn

Name _____

DIRECTIONS:
In each question the same word is divided into syllables in three different ways. Decide which is the correct way to divide the word and mark the answer.

1. ● re•peat ○ rep•eat ○ repe•at	7. ● swim•mer ○ sw•immer ○ swimm•er	13. ○ bla•ckboard ● black•board ○ blackb•oard
2. ● re•ply ○ rep•ly ○ repl•y	8. ○ pr•epare ● pre•pare ○ prep•are	14. ○ co•mplain ○ comp•lain ● com•plain
3. ○ fl•utter ○ flu•tter ● flut•ter	9. ○ tre•etop ● tree•top ○ treet•op	15. ○ e•xpert ● ex•pert ○ exp•ert
4. ○ r•eward ● re•ward ○ rew•ard	10. ● a•corn ○ ac•orn ○ aco•rn	16. ○ blu•ebird ○ blueb•ird ● blue•bird
5. ○ st•ation ● sta•tion ○ stat•ion	11. ○ be•rry ● ber•ry ○ berr•y	17. ● gold•fish ○ gol•dfish ○ goldf•ish
6. ○ se•aweed ○ seaw•eed ● sea•weed	12. ○ bugg•y ○ bu•ggy ● bug•gy	18. ○ ho•llow ○ holl•ow ● hol•low

Name _____

DIRECTIONS:
In each question the same word is divided into syllables in three different ways. Decide which is the correct way to divide the word and mark the answer.

1. ○ froz•en ● fro•zen ○ fr•ozen	7. ○ ta•lent ● tal•ent ○ tale•nt	13. ○ he•lmet ● hel•met ○ helm•et
2. ○ m•aple ● ma•ple ○ map•le	8. ● pri•vate ○ priv•ate ○ priva•te	14. ● po•lite ○ pol•ite ○ poli•te
3. ○ fli•pper ● flip•per ○ flipp•er	9. ○ pa•rent ● par•ent ○ pare•nt	15. ● per•form ○ perf•orm ○ perfo•rm
4. ○ m•edal ○ me•dal ● med•al	10. ○ st•udent ● stu•dent ○ stud•ent	16. ○ s•olid ○ so•lid ● sol•id
5. ● men•tion ○ ment•ion ○ me•ntion	11. ○ pa•ttern ● pat•tern ○ patt•ern	17. ○ ro•wboat ● row•boat ○ rowbo•at
6. ○ pa•ckage ○ pac•kage ● pack•age	12. ○ pu•nish ● pun•ish ○ puni•sh	18. ● re•ceive ○ rec•eive ○ rece•ive

Answer Key

Name _____

Skill: Syllabication

DIRECTIONS:
In each question the same word is divided into syllables in three different ways. Decide which is the correct way to divide the word and mark the answer.

1. ○ tr•umpet
   ● trum•pet
   ○ trump•et

2. ○ a•ddress
   ● ad•dress
   ○ add•ress

3. ○ bu•cket
   ○ buc•ket
   ● buck•et

4. ○ a•wful
   ● aw•ful
   ○ awf•ul

5. ● com•mand
   ○ co•mmand
   ○ comm•and

6. ● de•tail
   ○ det•ail
   ○ deta•il

7. ○ cu•rtain
   ● cur•tain
   ○ curt•ain

8. ● cac•tus
   ○ ca•ctus
   ○ cact•us

9. ● in•sect
   ○ ins•ect
   ○ inse•ct

10. ○ fre•edom
    ○ freed•om
    ● free•dom

11. ○ o•bject
    ● ob•ject
    ○ obj•ect

12. ○ harv•est
    ● har•vest
    ○ harve•st

13. ○ le•vel
    ● lev•el
    ○ leve•l

14. ● out•line
    ○ outl•ine
    ○ ou•tline

15. ○ gr•umpy
    ● grum•py
    ○ grump•y

16. ○ nec•klace
    ● neck•lace
    ○ neckl•ace

17. ○ pa•lace
    ● pal•ace
    ○ pala•ce

18. ○ sh•aggy
    ○ sha•ggy
    ● shag•gy

©Kelley Wingate CD 3735   13

Name _____

Skill: Syllabication

DIRECTIONS:
In each question the same word is divided into syllables in three different ways. Decide which is the correct way to divide the word and mark the answer.

1. ● re•main
   ○ rem•ain
   ○ rema•in

2. ○ pa•rtner
   ○ par•tner
   ● part•ner

3. ○ rep•lace
   ○ repl•ace
   ● re•place

4. ○ st•upid
   ● stu•pid
   ○ stup•id

5. ○ gra•ceful
   ○ gracef•ul
   ● grace•ful

6. ○ su•pply
   ○ supp•ly
   ● sup•ply

7. ● rail•road
   ○ railro•ad
   ○ rai•lroad

8. ○ po•wder
   ● pow•der
   ○ powd•er

9. ● pi•lot
   ○ p•ilot
   ○ pil•ot

10. ○ se•ttle
    ● set•tle
    ○ sett•le

11. ○ t•ulip
    ● tu•lip
    ○ tul•ip

12. ● air•port
    ○ airp•ort
    ○ ai•rport

13. ○ co•llar
    ○ coll•ar
    ● col•lar

14. ○ bi•scuit
    ○ bisc•uit
    ● bis•cuit

15. ○ bu•ndle
    ● bun•dle
    ○ bund•le

16. ○ excu•se
    ● ex•cuse
    ○ e•xcuse

17. ● con•fuse
    ○ co•nfuse
    ○ conf•use

18. ○ a•nger
    ● an•ger
    ○ ang•er

©Kelley Wingate CD 3735   14

Name _____

Skill: Syllabication

DIRECTIONS:
In each question the same word is divided into syllables in three different ways. Decide which is the correct way to divide the word and mark the answer.

1. ○ mi•stake
   ● mis•take
   ○ mist•ake

2. ○ hom•eade
   ○ homea•de
   ● home•ade

3. ○ ma•nger
   ● man•ger
   ○ mang•er

4. ○ mu•ddy
   ● mud•dy
   ○ mudd•y

5. ● hu•man
   ○ hum•an
   ○ h•uman

6. ○ gi•ggle
   ● gig•gle
   ○ gigg•le

7. ○ kin•gdom
   ● king•dom
   ○ kingd•om

8. ○ i•mprove
   ○ imp•rove
   ● im•prove

9. ○ pri•ncess
   ● prin•cess
   ○ princ•ess

10. ○ ta•ngle
    ○ tang•le
    ● tan•gle

11. ● pro•tect
    ○ prot•ect
    ○ pr•otect

12. ○ scatt•er
    ○ sca•tter
    ● scat•ter

13. ○ she•pherd
    ● shep•herd
    ○ sheph•erd

14. ○ su•ccess
    ● suc•cess
    ○ succ•ess

15. ○ re•scue
    ● res•cue
    ○ resc•ue

16. ○ surf•ace
    ○ su•rface
    ● sur•face

17. ○ se•ason
    ● sea•son
    ○ seas•on

18. ● ro•bin
    ○ rob•in
    ○ r•obin

©Kelley Wingate CD 3735   15

Name _____

Skill: Syllabication—Test 7

DIRECTIONS:
In each question the same word is divided into syllables in three different ways. Decide which is the correct way to divide the word and mark the answer.

1. ● six•teen
   ○ sixt•een
   ○ sixte•en

2. ○ sy•mbol
   ● sym•bol
   ○ symb•ol

3. ○ twent•y
   ○ twe•nty
   ● twen•ty

4. ● a•larm
   ○ al•arm
   ○ ala•rm

5. ● de•mand
   ○ dem•and
   ○ dema•nd

6. ○ co•mfort
   ● com•fort
   ○ comf•ort

7. ○ che•erful
   ○ chee•rful
   ● cheer•ful

8. ○ ba•ker
   ● bak•er
   ○ bake•r

9. ○ e•ager
   ● ea•ger
   ○ eag•er

10. ○ bar•nyard
    ● barn•yard
    ○ barny•ard

11. ○ hai•rcut
    ● hair•cut
    ○ haric•ut

12. ○ la•undry
    ○ lau•ndry
    ● laun•dry

13. ○ ho•oray
    ● hoo•ray
    ○ hoor•ay

14. ○ flas•hlight
    ● flash•light
    ○ flashl•ight

15. ○ hu•nger
    ● hun•ger
    ○ hung•er

16. ○ li•quid
    ● liq•uid
    ○ liqu•id

17. ● na•ture
    ○ nat•ure
    ○ natur•e

18. ○ pr•event
    ● pre•vent
    ○ prev•ent

© Carson-Dellosa CD-3735   16

©Kelley Wingate CD 3735   108

Answer Key

DIRECTIONS:
In each question the same word is divided into syllables in three different ways. Decide which is the correct way to divide the word and mark the answer.

1. ○ sa•ddle / ● sad•dle / ○ sadd•le
2. ● safe•ty / ○ saf•ety / ○ sa•fety
3. ○ spr•inkle / ● sprin•kle / ○ sprink•le
4. ○ te•mper / ○ temp•er / ● tem•per
5. ● school•work / ○ scho•olwork / ○ schoolw•ork
6. ○ sho•elace / ○ shoel•ace / ● shoe•lace
7. ○ stai•rway / ○ sta•irway / ● stair•way
8. ● sur•round / ○ surr•ound / ○ su•rround
9. ○ pe•tal / ● pet•al / ○ peta•l
10. ○ som•eplace / ● some•place / ○ somepl•ace
11. ○ ru•bber / ● rub•ber / ○ rubb•er
12. ○ tra•ffic / ● traf•fic / ○ traff•ic
13. ○ u•nfair / ● un•fair / ○ unf•air
14. ● un•wrap / ○ unw•rap / ○ unwr•ap
15. ○ wi•ggle / ● wig•gle / ○ wigg•le
16. ● camp•fire / ○ cam•pfire / ○ campfi•re
17. ○ ben•eath / ○ bene•ath / ● be•neath
18. ● day•dream / ○ daydr•eam / ○ daydre•am

©Kelley Wingate CD 3735   17

DIRECTIONS:
In each question the same word is divided into syllables in three different ways. Decide which is the correct way to divide the word and mark the answer.

1. ○ car•dboard / ● card•board / ○ cardbo•ard
2. ○ ve•lvet / ● vel•vet / ○ velv•et
3. ○ wo•bble / ○ wobb•le / ● wob•ble
4. ○ ce•llar / ● cel•lar / ○ cell•ar
5. ○ ca•ptive / ● cap•tive / ○ capt•ive
6. ● di•rect / ○ dir•ect / ○ dire•ct
7. ● cot•tage / ○ cott•age / ○ cotta•ge
8. ○ wa•lrus / ○ walr•us / ● wal•rus
9. ○ wrink•le / ○ wri•nkle / ● wrin•kle
10. ○ cent•ral / ● cen•tral / ○ ce•ntral
11. ○ di•sturb / ● dis•turb / ○ dist•urb
12. ○ ba•rrel / ● bar•rel / ○ barr•el
13. ● fan•cy / ○ fa•ncy / ○ fanc•y
14. ● wa•ter•fall / ○ wat•erf•all / ○ wa•terf•all
15. ○ fe•llow / ● fel•low / ○ fell•ow
16. ● be•have / ○ beh•ave / ○ behav•e
17. ○ a•ppear / ● ap•pear / ○ app•ear
18. ○ clo•set / ○ close•t / ● clos•et

©Kelley Wingate CD 3735   18

DIRECTIONS:
Read each group of words. Mark the one that is **not** spelled correctly.

1. ○ able / ○ anyone / ○ beside / ● buny / ○ clap
2. ● deside / ○ eight / ○ five / ○ golden / ○ hundred
3. ○ lay / ○ meant / ○ none / ○ pen / ● probabbly
4. ○ root / ○ she'll / ● somhow / ○ tie / ○ village
5. ● wemen / ○ zoom / ○ wolf / ○ vegetable / ○ tickle
6. ○ sudden / ○ sold / ○ she'd / ○ rooster / ● prise
7. ○ peek / ○ nod / ● medow / ○ late / ○ goat
8. ○ fit / ○ egg / ● deare / ○ circus / ○ bunch
9. ○ bend / ● anymor / ○ watch / ○ someone / ○ note
10. ○ hole / ○ done / ○ bark / ● trik / ○ place
11. ○ into / ○ put / ○ turtle / ● becuase / ○ drink
12. ○ horse / ○ onle / ○ soon / ○ wet / ○ anyway
13. ○ bet / ○ burn / ● clasroom / ○ deep / ○ either
14. ○ flap / ○ goodness / ○ hung / ○ lead / ● meassure
15. ○ noon / ● pensil / ○ problem / ○ rose / ○ she's

©Kelley Wingate CD 3735   19

DIRECTIONS:
Read each group of words. Mark the one that is **not** spelled correctly.

1. ○ somewhere / ○ suit / ● tite / ○ vine / ○ won
2. ○ yourself / ○ woke / ○ van / ● Thirsday / ○ such
3. ○ soil / ○ sharp / ● rouf / ○ print / ○ peanut
4. ○ nobody / ○ matter / ○ large / ○ huge / ● givn
5. ○ fishermen / ○ editor / ● daitime / ○ circle / ○ bump
6. ○ bench / ○ anybody / ● was'nt / ○ someday / ○ nose
7. ● holde / ○ doesn't / ○ bake / ○ tree / ○ pick
8. ○ just / ○ rabbitt / ○ two / ○ been / ○ drove
9. ○ hungry / ○ our / ○ sorry / ○ what / ● anewhere
10. ○ between / ○ bush / ○ clay / ○ deer / ● elefant
11. ● flach / ○ gotten / ○ hunt / ○ leaf / ○ meat
12. ○ north / ○ penny / ○ promise / ● rouff / ○ sheet
13. ○ son / ● sumer / ○ till / ○ visit / ○ wonder
14. ○ young / ● wize / ○ valley / ○ thunder / ○ stuff
15. ○ soft / ○ share / ○ roller / ● prinse / ○ pea

©Kelley Wingate CD 3735   20

Answer Key

Page 21

Name _____ Skill: Spelling

DIRECTIONS:
Read each group of words. Mark the one that is **not** spelled correctly.

1. ○ nine / ○ mask / ○ lap / ○ hug / ● gaint
2. ○ finish / ● edje / ○ daylight / ○ choose / ○ built
3. ○ belt / ○ answer / ○ use / ○ snow / ● noyse
4. ○ high / ○ doctor / ○ ate / ○ top / ● poeple
5. ○ pat / ○ took / ● aroind / ○ dinner / ○ herself
6. ○ nice / ○ snake / ● untill / ○ angry / ○ below
7. ○ beyond / ● buzy / ○ clear / ○ desk / ○ elevator
8. ○ flat / ○ grab / ● huntor / ○ lean / ○ meet
9. ○ notice / ○ pepper / ● proude / ○ round / ○ shell
10. ○ soup / ○ Sunday / ○ tinkle / ● voyce / ○ wonderful
11. ○ you've / ○ wire / ○ upstairs / ○ thump / ● stroong
12. ○ sock / ○ shape / ○ roll / ● pretind / ○ pay
13. ● newspapper / ○ marry / ○ language / ○ howl / ○ ghost
14. ○ finger / ○ eaten / ● daugter / ○ chirp / ○ buildings
15. ○ belong / ● aliso / ○ smiled / ○ never / ○ zoo

©Kelley Wingate CD 3735   21

Page 22

Name _____ Skill: Spelling

DIRECTIONS:
Read each group of words. Mark the one that is **not** spelled correctly.

1. ● helpper / ○ dark / ○ aren't / ○ today / ○ park
2. ○ lake / ○ ran / ○ us / ● beggin / ○ ever
3. ● Iv'e / ○ paint / ○ squirrel / ○ while / ○ apartment
4. ○ bill / ● buter / ○ clever / ○ detective / ○ else
5. ○ flew / ○ grade / ○ hurry / ● leep / ○ melt
6. ● nowwhere / ○ perfect / ○ prove / ○ row / ○ shine
7. ○ space / ○ sunny / ○ tiptoe / ● waggon / ○ wool
8. ○ you'll / ○ winner / ○ upside / ● thumbe / ○ stripe
9. ○ soap / ○ shall / ○ rode / ○ press / ● paaw
10. ○ net / ● marcket / ○ land / ○ hour / ○ graph
11. ○ final / ● eazy / ○ dash / ○ chin / ○ build
12. ○ bell / ○ already / ● tirn / ○ smile / ○ near
13. ○ heard / ○ dance / ○ apple / ○ three / ● papper
14. ○ last / ○ road / ○ very / ○ being / ● everone
15. ○ inside / ○ pan / ● staind / ○ white / ○ arm

©Kelley Wingate CD 3735   22

Page 23

Name _____ Skill: Spelling

DIRECTIONS:
Read each group of words. Mark the one that is **not** spelled correctly.

1. ● blackbery / ○ butterfly / ○ click / ○ die / ○ elves
2. ○ flip / ○ grandfather / ○ I'd / ● leern / ○ meow
3. ○ number / ○ person / ○ puff / ○ rub / ● shiney
4. ○ spaceship / ○ super / ● tood / ○ wake / ○ world
5. ● yo'ud / ○ wink / ○ upset / ○ throw / ○ string
6. ○ sniff / ○ shake / ○ robber / ○ present / ● pathe
7. ○ nest / ○ mark / ○ lady / ○ hospital / ● gease
8. ○ fight / ○ east / ○ dandelion / ○ child / ● bugg
9. ● beleive / ○ almost / ○ try / ○ smell / ○ named
10. ○ hear / ● cri / ○ anything / ○ thought / ○ over
11. ○ laugh / ○ rock / ○ walt / ○ best / ● evereything
12. ● isnt / ○ part / ○ star / ○ wind / ○ arrow
13. ○ blanket / ○ climb / ○ button / ● diferent / ○ empty
14. ○ float / ● grandmoher / ○ ice / ○ leather / ○ message
15. ○ nut / ○ phone / ○ pull / ● rouler / ○ ship

©Kelley Wingate CD 3735   23

Page 24

Name _____ Skill: Spelling

DIRECTIONS:
Read each group of words. Mark the one that is **not** spelled correctly.

1. ○ speak / ○ supper / ○ toast / ○ wall / ● worme
2. ○ yet / ○ wing / ● uppon / ○ throughout / ○ strike
3. ○ sneaker / ● shaddow / ○ roar / ○ practice / ○ patch
4. ● neiter / ○ march / ○ ladder / ○ hose / ○ gather
5. ● feild / ○ earth / ○ damp / ○ chief / ○ brush
6. ○ behind / ○ alley / ○ trip / ○ six / ● miself
7. ○ he's / ● could'nt / ○ ant / ○ there / ○ or
8. ○ liked / ● sade / ○ walk / ○ better / ○ everywhere
9. ○ jay / ○ party / ○ start / ● wintter / ○ art
10. ● bleew / ○ buy / ○ clock / ○ dig / ○ enemy
11. ○ flood / ○ gray / ○ idea / ○ led / ● mett
12. ○ o'clock / ○ piano / ○ puppy / ● runer / ○ shirt
13. ● specal / ○ suppose / ○ toe / ○ wander / ○ worn
14. ○ year / ○ win / ● untye / ○ through / ○ stretch
15. ○ snap / ● shaep / ○ river / ○ pour / ○ paste

©Kelley Wingate CD 3735   24

Answer Key

DIRECTIONS:
Read each group of words. Mark the one that is **not** spelled correctly.

1. ○ neighbor
   ○ map
   ○ known
   ○ horn
   ● gat

2. ○ few
   ● eirly
   ○ daddy
   ○ chicken
   ○ brought

3. ○ before
   ○ alike
   ○ tried
   ● sisster
   ○ moved

4. ○ head
   ○ country
   ● aney
   ○ think
   ○ other

5. ○ lion
   ○ same
   ○ was
   ● bicke
   ○ eye

6. ○ keep
   ● pickture
   ○ stay
   ○ wish
   ○ artist

7. ● blok
   ○ cage
   ○ cloth
   ○ dine
   ○ enough

8. ○ flour
   ○ growl
   ○ important
   ● leeft
   ○ mice

9. ● osean
   ○ picnic
   ○ purple
   ○ rush
   ○ shook

10. ○ spell
    ○ swam
    ● tommorow
    ○ warm
    ○ worry

11. ○ yard
    ● wiffe
    ○ unhappy
    ○ though
    ○ straw

12. ○ smoke
    ○ seven
    ○ ring
    ● pottato
    ○ past

13. ○ neck
    ○ lying
    ○ knot
    ○ hope
    ● gardan

14. ○ fence
    ○ ear
    ○ curl
    ○ chew
    ● brooke

15. ○ bedtime
    ● airplaine
    ○ train
    ○ sign
    ○ move

DIRECTIONS:
Read each group of words. Mark the one that is **not** spelled correctly.

1. ○ hand
   ○ cook
   ● anather
   ○ then
   ○ open

2. ○ live
   ○ sat
   ○ water
   ● birthday
   ○ face

3. ○ kind
   ○ plan
   ○ step
   ○ without
   ● assleep

4. ○ bloom
   ○ camp
   ● cornor
   ○ dirt
   ○ enter

5. ○ fold
   ○ frown
   ● indede
   ○ lemon
   ○ middle

6. ● ofice
   ○ pie
   ○ purr
   ○ rustle
   ○ shoot

7. ○ spend
   ● sweete
   ○ tool
   ○ wash
   ○ worth

8. ○ wrote
   ○ wide
   ○ understood
   ○ third
   ● stranjer

9. ○ silly
   ○ set
   ○ rid
   ● pokket
   ○ pass

10. ○ nearby
    ○ main
    ● knoock
    ○ honey
    ○ garbage

11. ○ felt
    ○ dust
    ○ cup
    ○ chest
    ● brocken

12. ○ blow
    ● kandle
    ○ clue
    ○ dish
    ○ evening

13. ○ follow
    ● hapen
    ○ indoor
    ○ lesson
    ○ mile

14. ○ often
    ○ pile
    ● quak
    ○ safe
    ○ short

15. ○ spent
    ○ swing
    ○ toss
    ○ wave
    ● would'nt

DIRECTIONS:
Read each group of words. Mark the one that is **not** spelled correctly.

1. ● written
   ○ whole
   ○ understand
   ○ thin
   ○ strange

2. ○ smart
   ● sentnce
   ○ rich
   ○ porch
   ○ parrot

3. ○ nail
   ● majic
   ○ knee
   ○ hit
   ○ gallop

4. ○ feelings
   ● durning
   ○ crow
   ○ cherry
   ○ broke

5. ● baord
   ○ candy
   ○ copy
   ○ dive
   ○ explain

6. ○ fool
   ○ hate
   ● intrest
   ○ lick
   ○ miller

7. ● liberry
   ○ instead
   ○ key
   ○ lunchroom
   ○ junk

8. ○ oil
   ● pillow
   ○ queen
   ○ sail
   ○ shot

9. ○ spill
   ○ swung
   ○ touch
   ● welcom
   ○ write

10. ○ whistle
    ○ truth
    ○ tent
    ● stomak
    ○ size

11. ○ seek
    ○ reach
    ● ponny
    ○ rainbow
    ○ ranch

12. ○ mouth
    ○ luck
    ○ jar
    ● Fryday
    ○ hidden

13. ○ fear
    ○ favorite
    ○ change
    ○ cowboy
    ● brase

14. ○ beach
    ● afriad
    ○ baby
    ○ backyard
    ○ fresh

15. ○ joke
    ○ drive
    ● crake
    ○ hammer
    ○ forget

DIRECTIONS:
Read the sentences and choices below. Mark the word or phrase that means almost the same thing as the word or phrase that is underlined in the sentence.

1. I worked very hard and now my muscles <u>ache</u>.

   ○ are soft
   ○ smell
   ● are sore

2. I want to own a large house when I am an <u>adult</u>.

   ○ teenager
   ● grown-up
   ○ doctor

3. I will <u>aid</u> you in your search for your missing dog.

   ○ call
   ○ find
   ● help

4. The <u>warning</u> bell let us know it was time to leave the ship.

   ○ loud
   ● alarm
   ○ captain's

5. Please <u>allow</u> me to carry that heavy box for you.

   ● let
   ○ help
   ○ watch

5. Is this the <u>actual</u> chair in which Abraham Lincoln sat?

   ○ only
   ● real
   ○ pretty

7. Joe will read the book now and answer the questions <u>afterward</u>.

   ○ first
   ○ tomorrow
   ● later

8. My <u>aim</u> is to be the best football player in this school!

   ● goal
   ○ shot
   ○ fast

9. My great grandmother is 101 and still <u>alive</u>!

   ○ dancing
   ○ happy
   ● living

10. The loose dog did not <u>appear</u> to be coming any closer.

    ○ want
    ● seem
    ○ run

Answer Key

Worksheet (page 29)

Name _____

Skill: Synonyms

DIRECTIONS:
Read the sentences and choices below. Mark the word or phrase that means almost the same thing as the word or phrase that is underlined in the sentence.

1. I could hear the train coming as I <u>approached</u> the tracks.
   - ○ backed away from
   - ○ looked at
   - ● neared

2. The <u>author</u> of this book is a friend of mine.
   - ○ artist
   - ● writer
   - ○ owner

3. Which <u>street</u> do I take to get to your house?
   - ○ bus
   - ○ turn
   - ● road

4. I do not want to <u>battle</u> with you.
   - ○ eat
   - ○ play
   - ● fight

5. Is that a <u>beetle</u> under that leaf?
   - ○ rock
   - ○ snake
   - ● bug

6. At what time did you <u>arrive</u>?
   - ○ leave
   - ● come
   - ○ get up

7. In <u>autumn</u>, the leaves turn red and yellow.
   - ● fall
   - ○ spring
   - ○ a month

8. I feel <u>awful</u> because I broke your baseball bat.
   - ○ silly
   - ○ glad
   - ● bad

9. The biggest <u>beast</u> in the zoo was the elephant.
   - ● animal
   - ○ show
   - ○ surprise

10. I <u>beg</u> you to let me have a pet parrot!
   - ○ want
   - ● ask
   - ○ tell

©Kelley Wingate CD 3735   29

Worksheet (page 30)

Name _____

Skill: Synonyms

DIRECTIONS:
Read the sentences and choices below. Mark the word or phrase that means almost the same thing as the word or phrase that is underlined in the sentence.

1. Can you see what is <u>beneath</u> that pile of boxes?
   - ○ in
   - ● under
   - ○ behind

2. Joel likes to <u>boast</u> about all his first place ribbons and medals.
   - ● brag
   - ○ tell
   - ○ flash

3. <u>Brake</u> the car when you come to a corner.
   - ○ hurry
   - ○ start
   - ● stop

4. Dad asked Jack to <u>cut</u> down that old oak tree in the yard.
   - ○ push
   - ● chop
   - ○ knock

5. Nan will <u>creep</u> across the floor and scare Jane.
   - ○ sweep
   - ○ dash
   - ● crawl

6. The <u>blaze</u> burned the whole store before it was put it out.
   - ○ sun
   - ○ heat
   - ● fire

7. The boxes were <u>bound</u> tightly and I couldn't open any of them.
   - ○ piled
   - ● wrapped
   - ○ pushed

8. <u>Cast</u> your fishing line into that deep water under the bridge.
   - ● throw
   - ○ drop
   - ○ trim

9. Can Sue <u>complete</u> her paper by next Tuesday?
   - ○ hand in
   - ○ start
   - ● finish

10. That job was not so <u>difficult</u> to do!
   - ○ easy
   - ● hard
   - ○ awful

©Kelley Wingate CD 3735   30

Worksheet (page 31)

Name _____

Skill: Synonyms

DIRECTIONS:
Read the sentences and choices below. Mark the word or phrase that means almost the same thing as the word or phrase that is underlined in the sentence.

1. There are <u>a dozen</u> eggs in the bowl.
   - ○ cracked
   - ● twelve
   - ○ broken

2. I was so surprised, I thought I might <u>pass out</u>!
   - ○ yell
   - ○ freeze
   - ● faint

3. We could see the new car <u>gleaming</u> in the parking lot.
   - ● shining
   - ○ running
   - ○ driving

4. We used a <u>hollow</u> tube for the experiment.
   - ○ round
   - ○ straw
   - ● empty

5. Which jar has the <u>least</u> amount of candy?
   - ○ greatest
   - ○ fattest
   - ● smallest

6. Mom can <u>dye</u> this white shirt and make it brown.
   - ● color
   - ○ mess up
   - ○ wash

7. Rosie <u>flung</u> the newspaper into the trash can.
   - ○ carried
   - ● tossed
   - ○ dumped

8. Bob is really a good <u>guy</u> because he is always helping people.
   - ○ cat
   - ● man
   - ○ female

9. I can tie my shoes <u>in an instant</u>!
   - ○ tightly
   - ○ slowly
   - ● quickly

10. The <u>motion</u> of the boat on the waves made me feel a little ill.
   - ● movement
   - ○ sound
   - ○ smell

©Kelley Wingate CD 3735   31

Worksheet (page 32)

Name _____

Skill: Synonyms—Test 5

DIRECTIONS:
Read the sentences and choices below. Mark the word or phrase that means almost the same thing as the word or phrase that is underlined in the sentence.

1. Get the <u>oars</u> for the boat.
   - ○ sails
   - ○ fishing poles
   - ● paddles

2. We can carry the water in that small <u>bucket</u>.
   - ● pail
   - ○ glass
   - ○ shovel

3. Will you <u>consider</u> giving me your skates when you get new ones?
   - ○ promise
   - ● think about
   - ○ throw away

4. The room was <u>dim</u> and cold.
   - ○ dirty
   - ○ freezing
   - ● unlit

5. You sing the words to the song and I will <u>echo</u> you.
   - ○ watch
   - ○ listen to
   - ● repeat

6. Sally is a quiet and <u>timid</u> girl.
   - ○ tall
   - ● shy
   - ○ clever

7. I have a <u>task</u> to do before I can come out and play.
   - ● chore
   - ○ game
   - ○ book

8. That <u>crook</u> just took my purse!
   - ○ bird
   - ○ gust of wind
   - ● thief

9. Help me <u>drag</u> this box to the garage.
   - ○ carry
   - ● pull
   - ○ unpack

10. That jewel might look pretty, but it is <u>a fake</u>!
   - ● not real
   - ○ a lot of money
   - ○ broken

© Carson-Dellosa CD-3735   32

Answer Key

Name _____

DIRECTIONS:
Read the sentences and choices below. Mark the word or phrase that means almost the same thing as the word or phrase that is underlined in the sentence.

1. Be careful driving because it is a <u>misty</u> morning.
- ● foggy
- ○ dry
- ○ nice

2. When I hold up my hand you must <u>halt</u>!
- ○ begin
- ○ run
- ● stop

3. Did you <u>invent</u> this wonderful new toy?
- ○ play with
- ● make
- ○ unwrap

4. I am hungry so I will <u>munch</u> these crackers for awhile.
- ○ borrow
- ○ hold
- ● chew

5. The captain will <u>steer</u> the ship safely to the dock.
- ○ tow
- ○ sink
- ● drive

6. Sharon peeked into the <u>gloom</u>, but could see nothing.
- ○ water
- ● darkness
- ○ sunshine

7. There was an <u>awful</u> storm coming our way.
- ● terrible
- ○ huge
- ○ puffy

8. If we keep the boat <u>level</u>, it won't tip over.
- ● even
- ○ empty
- ○ here

9. I am tired and need to <u>pause</u> for a moment.
- ○ sleep
- ● wait
- ○ breathe

10. What is that big <u>bundle</u> Kelly is carrying?
- ● package
- ○ sheet
- ○ tray

Name _____

DIRECTIONS:
Read the sentences and choices below. Mark the word or phrase that means almost the same thing as the word or phrase that is underlined in the sentence.

1. These new cards did not cost me a <u>cent</u>!
- ○ dollar
- ○ nickel
- ● penny

2. Will you <u>continue</u> working while I answer the telephone?
- ○ quit
- ● keep on
- ○ busy

3. My <u>dime</u> fell out of my pocket and rolled across the floor.
- ○ pencil
- ○ watch
- ● ten cents

4. Shut off the <u>engine</u> when you put in the gas.
- ● motor
- ○ wind
- ○ oven

5. I felt very <u>foolish</u> carrying an umbrella on a sunny day!
- ○ comfortable
- ○ hot
- ● silly

6. I began to <u>chuckle</u> when I heard the news.
- ○ cry
- ● laugh
- ○ frown

7. Naomi <u>crushed</u> the flowers when she stuffed them in the bag.
- ● smashed
- ○ protected
- ○ cut

8. The spook house was a <u>dreadful</u> place to spend the night!
- ○ wonderful
- ● awful
- ○ strange

9. The answers to this test are either true or <u>false</u>.
- ○ given
- ● not true
- ○ correct

10. Dad said to use <u>glue</u> to hold the sticks together.
- ○ nails
- ● paste
- ○ rope

Name _____

DIRECTIONS:
Read the sentences and choices below. Mark the word or phrase that means almost the same thing as the word or phrase that is underlined in the sentence.

1. Frank is the <u>champion</u> marble player in our club.
- ● best
- ○ worst
- ○ oldest

2. Can you <u>discover</u> the answer to my question?
- ○ work
- ○ tell
- ● find

3. Did you <u>enjoy</u> the movie?
- ○ watch
- ○ go to
- ● like

4. Katrina wore a beautiful <u>gown</u> to the dance.
- ○ crown
- ● dress
- ○ coat

5. The bee will not <u>harm</u> you if you stand still.
- ● hurt
- ○ buzz
- ○ scare

6. You could hear the school bell <u>ring</u> two blocks away.
- ○ circle
- ● clang
- ○ shout

7. The boat began to <u>drift</u> away because we didn't tie it to the dock.
- ● wander
- ○ wonder
- ○ row

8. The child was <u>fearful</u> that his mother was leaving.
- ● afraid
- ○ yelling
- ○ happy

9. The hunter lived in a small <u>cottage</u> in the woods.
- ○ place
- ○ tent
- ● cabin

10. Chrissy likes to <u>chatter</u> too much!
- ○ eat
- ● talk
- ○ play

Name _____

DIRECTIONS:
Read the sentences and choices below. Mark the word or phrase that means almost the same thing as the word or phrase that is underlined in the sentence.

1. The clothesline began to <u>droop</u> and the clothes got dirty.
- ○ break
- ● sag
- ○ bounce

2. Will you please <u>clip</u> the bushes by the front sidewalk?
- ○ shape
- ○ water
- ● trim

3. An <u>enormous</u> storm cloud was headed toward the lake.
- ○ dark
- ○ scary
- ● huge

4. Will you please <u>fetch</u> me a cool glass of water?
- ○ throw
- ● get
- ○ drink

5. You may have <u>a couple</u> of those cookies after school.
- ○ five
- ● two
- ○ ten

6. The bird built a <u>snug</u> nest for her seven blue eggs.
- ● cozy
- ○ high
- ○ big

7. We waded in the <u>stream</u> to cool our feet.
- ● creek
- ○ shade
- ○ tall grass

8. Father <u>commanded</u> me to pick up the tools I had been using.
- ○ asked
- ● ordered
- ○ begged

9. We waited until <u>dawn</u> before leaving the house.
- ○ evening
- ○ midnight
- ● morning

10. Do you have a good <u>grip</u> on the box so it won't fall?
- ● hold
- ○ ribbon
- ○ knee

Answer Key

Page 37

Name _____   Skill: Antonyms

DIRECTIONS:
Read the sentences and choices below. Mark the word that means the opposite of the word that is underlined in the sentence.

1. I am sorry I broke the vase. It was an <u>accident</u>.
- ○ clumsy
- ● on purpose
- ○ wrong

2. Let's go to the movie and eat <u>afterward</u>.
- ○ later
- ● before
- ○ dinner

3. I was <u>alarmed</u> when I heard the door open.
- ○ upset
- ○ scared
- ● calm

4. Please read this page <u>silently</u> then answer the questions.
- ○ to yourself
- ○ openly
- ● aloud

5. That car is really <u>ancient</u>!
- ○ old
- ● new
- ○ rusty

6. I have the <u>actual</u> ball used in the big game!
- ● false
- ○ orange
- ○ signed

7. That <u>child</u> should not be standing in the street.
- ○ baby
- ○ boy
- ● adult

8. I think that fish by the rock is <u>dead</u>.
- ● alive
- ○ not breathing
- ○ silver

9. I was <u>amazed</u> when I watched the magic show.
- ● bored
- ○ happy
- ○ scared

10. After a warm shower, I felt <u>terrific</u>!
- ○ comfortable
- ○ clean
- ● awful

©Kelley Wingate CD 3735   37

Page 38

Name _____   Skill: Antonyms

DIRECTIONS:
Read the sentences and choices below. Mark the word that means the opposite of the word that is underlined in the sentence.

1. Do you think these drapes will <u>darken</u> the room?
- ○ shade
- ○ cover
- ● brighten

2. I am <u>confused</u> about what I should do next.
- ○ mixed up
- ● sure
- ○ afraid

3. That car is <u>enormous</u>!
- ○ huge
- ○ shiny
- ● tiny

4. Peter began to <u>frown</u> when it started to rain.
- ● grin
- ○ worry
- ○ grow

5. Did the dog <u>uncover</u> that bone in my backyard?
- ○ chew
- ○ dig up
- ● bury

6. I will <u>warm</u> the chocolate before we put it on the cookies.
- ○ heat
- ● chill
- ○ eat

7. Did you <u>lose</u> your book?
- ● find
- ○ misplace
- ○ hide

8. Do you think the answer is <u>true</u>?
- ○ good
- ○ real
- ● false

9. I <u>slept</u> when I heard the gentle rain falling on the roof.
- ○ napped
- ○ looked
- ● awoke

10. Please <u>continue</u> when you hear the bell.
- ● stop
- ○ go on
- ○ begin

©Kelley Wingate CD 3735   38

Page 39

Name _____   Skill: Antonyms

DIRECTIONS:
Read the sentences and choices below. Mark the word that means the opposite of the word that is underlined in the sentence.

1. I like to take a walk at <u>dawn</u> because the sky is so pretty.
- ○ early
- ○ morning
- ● dusk

2. Janice wants a <u>fancy</u> dress for the party this Saturday.
- ○ frilly
- ● plain
- ○ pretty

3. Harvey <u>happily</u> helped his mom bring in the heavy bags.
- ○ joyfully
- ● angrily
- ○ sweetly

4. George was <u>anxious</u> about taking the test on Friday.
- ○ scared
- ○ curious
- ● calm

5. Is this the <u>correct</u> way to fold a napkin?
- ○ right
- ● wrong
- ○ useful

6. Please stand <u>at a distance</u> while I cut this log.
- ○ over there
- ● close
- ○ far away

7. Is the ice cube <u>frozen</u>?
- ● melted
- ○ icy
- ○ square

8. I can ride my bike <u>backward</u> over the bridge.
- ○ slowly
- ○ quickly
- ● forward

9. The bird had many <u>colorful</u> feathers on its wings.
- ● dull
- ○ fluffy
- ○ bright

10. Do not <u>drag</u> your bookbag across the floor.
- ○ throw
- ● push
- ○ lift

©Kelley Wingate CD 3735   39

Page 40

Name _____   Skill: Antonyms—Test 4

DIRECTIONS:
Read the sentences and choices below. Mark the word that means the opposite of the word that is underlined in the sentence.

1. Is this the <u>entrance</u> to the circus?
- ○ door
- ○ way in
- ● exit

2. Are we any <u>closer</u>?
- ○ nearer
- ○ drier
- ● further

3. The cups are on the shelf <u>above</u> the plates.
- ○ on top
- ● beneath
- ○ over

4. Mark was <u>upset</u> when the dog sat on his lap.
- ○ angry
- ○ unhappy
- ● comforted

5. The math problems for today were so <u>easy</u> to finish.
- ○ not hard
- ○ slow
- ● difficult

6. Jose told his friend <u>farewell</u>.
- ○ goodbye
- ● hello
- ○ good luck

7. I can't believe that you can just <u>disappear</u> like that!
- ● show up
- ○ go away
- ○ hide

8. That is the biggest <u>mountain</u> I have ever seen.
- ○ hill
- ○ river
- ● canyon

9. I will <u>creep</u> along the road until that strange car is gone.
- ● speed
- ○ crawl
- ○ whisper

10. Ricky thought the play we saw was <u>wonderful</u>!
- ○ colorful
- ● dreadful
- ○ very good

© Carson-Dellosa CD-3735   40

Answer Key

Name _____ Skill: Antonyms—Test 5

DIRECTIONS:
Read the sentences and choices below. Mark the word that means the opposite of the word that is underlined in the sentence.

1. We each have <u>equal</u> stacks of baseball cards.
   - ○ many
   - ○ even
   - ● uneven

2. We can find the answer to pollution if we look to the <u>future</u>.
   - ○ distance
   - ○ next day
   - ● past

3. I can keep my arm <u>bent</u> for several hours.
   - ● straight
   - ○ broken
   - ○ crooked

4. I did not feel <u>comfortable</u> in the large chair.
   - ○ easy
   - ● uneasy
   - ○ warm

5. Can you <u>deliver</u> the package today?
   - ○ bring
   - ● pick up
   - ○ open

6. I can be <u>brave</u> when I am alone in a strange place.
   - ● fearful
   - ○ fearless
   - ○ strong

7. What time will you <u>arrive</u>?
   - ○ come
   - ○ meet
   - ● leave

8. Daniel wanted to <u>free</u> the whale.
   - ○ let go
   - ○ cost
   - ● capture

9. The cookie was <u>crisp</u> and tasty.
   - ● soggy
   - ○ cracking
   - ○ sweet

10. Sometimes Larry thinks he is really <u>smart</u>!
   - ○ sharp
   - ○ clever
   - ● dumb

41

Name _____ Skill: Antonyms—Test 6

DIRECTIONS:
Read the sentences and choices below. Mark the word that means the opposite of the word that is underlined in the sentence.

1. The <u>girl</u> in the red shirt is my friend.
   - ○ lady
   - ● boy
   - ○ child

2. Ron was <u>proud</u> of the grade he got on his test.
   - ● ashamed
   - ○ pleased
   - ○ careful

3. I <u>beg</u> you to give me back my book.
   - ○ ask
   - ○ dare
   - ● command

4. Do not be so <u>timid</u> about meeting new people.
   - ○ afraid
   - ● eager
   - ○ angry

5. Do you think that tiger in the cage is <u>fierce</u>?
   - ○ angry
   - ○ wild
   - ● tame

6. I will <u>stare</u> when I see you.
   - ● look away
   - ○ gaze
   - ○ blink

7. We keep our old clothes and toys in the <u>cellar</u>.
   - ○ basement
   - ○ closet
   - ● attic

8. I think your new shoes are really <u>cute</u>!
   - ● ugly
   - ○ old
   - ○ pretty

9. I am <u>calm</u> when I think about going on a trip to the ocean.
   - ● excited
   - ○ quiet
   - ○ dreaming

10. I couldn't help but <u>grin</u> when I heard the news.
   - ○ smile
   - ● frown
   - ○ growl

42

Name _____ Skill: Antonyms

DIRECTIONS:
Read the sentences and choices below. Mark the word that means the opposite of the word that is underlined in the sentence.

1. Who was the <u>loser</u> of the race?
   - ○ worst
   - ○ happiest
   - ● champion

2. You should keep a <u>damp</u> cloth on the sore until it feels better.
   - ● dry
   - ○ wet
   - ○ cold

3. Will you say some words that might <u>encourage</u> me?
   - ○ help
   - ● discourage
   - ○ support

4. This pillow is too <u>soft</u>!
   - ○ comfortable
   - ● hard
   - ○ difficult

5. I <u>love</u> the color of leaves in the autumn.
   - ○ see
   - ● hate
   - ○ like

6. A coin like this one is <u>rare</u>.
   - ○ unusual
   - ○ costly
   - ● common

7. I could see a <u>bright</u> light at the end of the tunnel.
   - ○ shiny
   - ● dim
   - ○ yellow

8. The surprise party we gave last night was a huge <u>success</u>.
   - ○ smash
   - ○ mess
   - ● failure

9. The <u>adult</u> quietly closed the door.
   - ○ grown-up
   - ○ man
   - ● youngster

10. I would like to <u>lend</u> a little help for this project.
   - ○ send
   - ○ give
   - ● borrow

43

Name _____ Skill: Antonyms

DIRECTIONS:
Read the sentences and choices below. Mark the word that means the opposite of the word that is underlined in the sentence.

1. We were <u>cheerful</u> when the game ended.
   - ● sad
   - ○ happy
   - ○ yelling

2. Is it <u>dangerous</u> to cross the street here?
   - ○ rare
   - ● safe
   - ○ allowed

3. I <u>hate</u> going to summer camp in the mountains.
   - ● enjoy
   - ○ don't like
   - ○ miss

4. Buying that car was a <u>foolish</u> thing to do.
   - ○ silly
   - ○ useless
   - ● wise

5. The <u>warmth</u> of the day felt good on my back.
   - ○ heat
   - ● coolness
   - ○ sun

6. Can you <u>complete</u> this project next week?
   - ○ finish
   - ● begin
   - ○ do

7. I am sure you will be <u>disappointed</u> if we watch that movie.
   - ○ angry
   - ○ unhappy
   - ● pleased

8. Is that a <u>real</u> beard your dad has?
   - ○ actual
   - ○ fuzzy
   - ● fake

9. You must speak in a <u>gentle</u> way if you expect your dog to listen.
   - ○ friendly
   - ○ soft
   - ● gruff

10. The hamburger was <u>tough</u> to chew.
   - ○ difficult
   - ○ hard
   - ● easy

44

115

Answer Key

Name _____

Skill: Antonyms

DIRECTIONS:
Read the sentences and choices below. Mark the word that means the opposite of the word that is underlined in the sentence.

1. Your name sounds <u>familiar</u> to me.
- ○ common
- ○ usual
- ● strange

2. Mark tried to <u>capture</u> the wild cat.
- ○ chase away
- ○ trap
- ● set free

3. I can <u>create</u> a whole city in my sandbox.
- ○ build
- ● destroy
- ○ pile

4. That orange is very <u>juicy</u>!
- ● dry
- ○ wet
- ○ tasty

5. I am <u>prepared</u> to give my report in class today.
- ○ thankful
- ● not ready
- ○ going

6. I <u>awaken</u> at eight each day.
- ● sleep
- ○ get up
- ○ stretch

7. Will you <u>fasten</u> the latch on the window?
- ● open
- ○ design
- ○ close

8. I <u>depend on</u> my sister to make my bed.
- ○ force
- ○ want
- ● don't need

9. Brian was a <u>naughty</u> boy today.
- ● good
- ○ bad
- ○ silly

10. The sleeve of my jacket is <u>torn</u>.
- ○ ripped
- ○ ragged
- ● mended

©Kelley Wingate CD 3735   45

Name _____

Skill: Vocabulary

DIRECTIONS:
Read the first part of the sentence and look at the underlined word or words. Choose the word or phrase that means about the same thing as the underlined word or phrase. Mark the correct answer.

1. A word that means to <u>pull on sharply</u> is ...
- ○ push
- ● yank
- ○ haul

2. To <u>believe that someone is honest, fair, and true</u> means ...
- ○ like
- ○ protect
- ● trust

3. A person who <u>will not give in or change</u> their mind is ...
- ○ smart
- ○ daydreaming
- ● stubborn

4. The word <u>simple</u> means ...
- ● easy
- ○ difficult
- ○ welcome

5. A person who <u>throws an angry fit</u> is in a ...
- ○ carriage
- ○ emergency
- ● rage

6. To <u>take something off</u> a truck or ship is to ...
- ○ load
- ○ erase
- ● unload

7. Another word for <u>chore or job</u> is ...
- ● task
- ○ test
- ○ declare

8. A person who <u>fights for a cause</u> is a ...
- ○ visitor
- ○ friend
- ● soldier

9. To <u>save someone from danger</u> is to ...
- ○ calm
- ● rescue
- ○ fault

10. When you <u>take tiny bites</u> of your food you ...
- ● nibble
- ○ delight
- ○ split

©Kelley Wingate CD 3735   46

Name _____

Skill: Vocabulary

DIRECTIONS:
Read the first part of the sentence and look at the underlined word or words. Choose the word or phrase that means about the same thing as the underlined word or phrase. Mark the correct answer.

1. Another word for <u>partner</u> is ...
- ○ self
- ○ passenger
- ● mate

2. A <u>safe place for boats and ships</u> is a ...
- ● harbor
- ○ waterfall
- ○ figure

3. When two things are <u>even or level</u>, they are ...
- ○ familiar
- ○ charming
- ● equal

4. To <u>come closer</u> is to ...
- ● approach
- ○ choke
- ○ exclaim

5. A <u>small stream</u> of water is a ...
- ○ layer
- ○ tickle
- ● trickle

6. A <u>long trip</u> is called a ...
- ○ thirst
- ○ symbol
- ● journey

7. To <u>sparkle and shine</u> is to ...
- ○ grumble
- ● glitter
- ○ cast

8. A <u>person who buys something</u> is a ...
- ● customer
- ○ costume
- ○ cactus

9. Something that is <u>rare</u> is ...
- ○ operate
- ● unusual
- ○ immediate

10. Something <u>used to look at things that are far away</u> is a ....
- ○ telephone
- ● telescope
- ○ headlights

©Kelley Wingate CD 3735   47

Name _____

Skill: Vocabulary

DIRECTIONS:
Read the first part of the sentence and look at the underlined word or words. Choose the word or phrase that means about the same thing as the underlined word or phrase. Mark the correct answer.

1. To <u>take the bends out</u> of is to ...
- ○ screech
- ○ position
- ● straighten

2. To <u>say again</u> is to ...
- ○ yawn
- ○ trace
- ● repeat

3. We <u>wear these to bed</u> at night ...
- ○ slippers
- ● pajamas
- ○ sleeves

4. <u>Clothes that are being washed</u> are ...
- ○ separate
- ○ liquid
- ● laundry

5. To <u>hurt someone or something</u> is to do ...
- ○ honor
- ○ cause
- ● harm

6. When we <u>cuddle</u> something, we ...
- ● snuggle
- ○ serve
- ○ stoop

7. Something that is <u>rapid</u> is ...
- ● fast
- ○ old
- ○ slow

8. When you <u>do as you are told</u>, you ...
- ○ roam
- ● obey
- ○ strain

9. To <u>give a clue</u> is to ...
- ● hint
- ○ form
- ○ glance

10. A <u>group of birds</u> is called a ...
- ○ business
- ● flock
- ○ future

©Kelley Wingate CD 3735   48

Answer Key

Page 49

Name _____

Skill: Vocabulary

DIRECTIONS:
Read the first part of the sentence and look at the underlined word or words. Choose the word or phrase that means about the same thing as the underlined word or phrase. Mark the correct answer.

1. When you give many details about something you...
- ● describe
- ○ rebel
- ○ cluster

2. What a balloon does when it pops ...
- ○ secure
- ○ locate
- ● burst

3. Something that is as bad as it gets is the ...
- ○ request
- ● worst
- ○ wept

4. To shake from fear or excitement is to ...
- ○ wheeze
- ● tremble
- ○ spear

5. Something that is excellent is ...
- ○ eerie
- ○ dainty
- ● splendid

6. Things put together into a set make a ...
- ○ complaint
- ● collection
- ○ corral

7. Something that covers and protects us is ...
- ○ shatter
- ○ mournful
- ● armor

8. Something that is common or everyday is ...
- ● usual
- ○ wisdom
- ○ speck

9. When you really want something to drink, you have ...
- ○ tradition
- ○ stake
- ● thirst

10. A person who is thin is usually called ...
- ● slim
- ○ definite
- ○ inspector

©Kelley Wingate CD 3735

49

Page 50

Name _____

Skill: Vocabulary—Test 5

DIRECTIONS:
Read the first part of each sentence and look at the underlined word or words. Choose the word or phrase that means about the same thing as the underlined word or phrase. Mark the correct answer.

1. To wash or clean by rubbing hard is to...
- ○ dimple
- ○ crumble
- ● scrub

2. When you get something you ...
- ○ reappear
- ○ navigate
- ● receive

3. Two things that are completely different are called...
- ○ onward
- ● opposite
- ○ mischief

4. Anything that happened before now is the...
- ○ future
- ● past
- ○ native

5. To make a person do something he doesn't want to do is to...
- ● force
- ○ outwit
- ○ link

6. When you stay behind you...
- ● remain
- ○ hitch
- ○ express

7. A group of related sentences is a...
- ● paragraph
- ○ sniffle
- ○ mission

8. The smallest amount is the...
- ○ rate
- ○ mutter
- ● least

9. To be thankful is to be...
- ○ necessary
- ○ sloppy
- ● grateful

10. A book that lists the meaning of words is a...
- ○ marvel
- ○ represent
- ● dictionary

© Carson-Dellosa CD-3735

50

Page 51

Name _____

Skill: Vocabulary

DIRECTIONS:
Read the first part of the sentence and look at the underlined word or words. Choose the word or phrase that means about the same thing as the underlined word or phrase. Mark the correct answer.

1. To order someone to do something is a ...
- ○ trough
- ● command
- ○ suggestion

2. A person who helps another is an ...
- ○ accident
- ○ adult
- ● assistant

3. Something that is very expensive or dear to you is a ...
- ○ centimeter
- ○ assembly
- ● treasure

4. To splash drops of water is to ...
- ○ shed
- ○ combine
- ● sprinkle

5. A part of something is a ...
- ○ cloak
- ● section
- ○ fashion

6. A person who is unable to see is ...
- ○ solemn
- ● blind
- ○ witness

7. To shake back and forth, almost falling down is to ...
- ○ overflow
- ○ concern
- ● wobble

8. A person who is quiet and shy is often called ...
- ● timid
- ○ constant
- ○ rumpled

9. A dog or cat with long, uneven hair is ...
- ○ countless
- ○ sensible
- ● shaggy

10. When you say you will not do something, you ...
- ● refuse
- ○ direct
- ○ crouch

©Kelley Wingate CD 3735

51

Page 52

Name _____

Skill: Vocabulary

DIRECTIONS:
Read the first part of the sentence and look at the underlined word or words. Choose the word or phrase that means about the same thing as the underlined word or phrase. Mark the correct answer.

1. To get ready is to ...
- ● prepare
- ○ invent
- ○ extend

2. When you are very unhappy you are ...
- ○ honest
- ● miserable
- ○ darling

3. A person who wants everything and doesn't share is ...
- ○ harmless
- ○ barefoot
- ● greedy

4. A person who is very devout is ...
- ● faithful
- ○ disappointed
- ○ independent

5. To watch and listen closely is to give your ...
- ● attention
- ○ disgust
- ○ launch

6. A short stop or break is a ...
- ○ kindness
- ○ jersey
- ● pause

7. To be flat or even is ...
- ○ humble
- ● level
- ○ grim

8. A person who is the best at what he does is an ...
- ● expert
- ○ octopus
- ○ ingredient

9. A child of your aunt or uncle is your ...
- ○ brother
- ○ headache
- ● cousin

10. A stiff hair on the face of a cat or dog is a ...
- ○ whisper
- ● whisker
- ○ gland

©Kelley Wingate CD 3735

52

Answer Key

Name _____

Skill: Vocabulary

DIRECTIONS:
Read the first part of the sentence and look at the underlined word or words. Choose the word or phrase that means about the same thing as the underlined word or phrase. Mark the correct answer.

1. A person who is a <u>guest</u> is a ...
- ○ tradition
- ○ volunteer
- ● visitor

2. <u>Drops of water that fall from your skin</u> when you are hot are ...
- ○ faucet
- ● sweat
- ○ itch

3. To <u>wander without purpose</u> is to ...
- ○ horrify
- ○ display
- ● roam

4. A person who is <u>well liked</u> by many other people is ...
- ○ advanced
- ● popular
- ○ painful

5. <u>As far as you can go</u> is the ...
- ○ current
- ○ deserve
- ● limit

6. <u>People, cars, trucks, and buses coming and going</u> are ...
- ○ haul
- ● traffic
- ○ desperate

7. Something that is <u>not very deep</u> is ...
- ● shallow
- ○ rhythmic
- ○ lagoon

8. To <u>stop something from happening</u> is to ...
- ○ caress
- ○ conduct
- ● prevent

9. Something <u>new and up to date</u> is ...
- ○ antique
- ○ grizzly
- ● modern

10. Something that is <u>not real</u> is ...
- ● imaginary
- ○ glossy
- ○ dignified

©Kelley Wingate CD 3735   53

Name _____

Skill: Vocabulary

DIRECTIONS:
Read the first part of the sentence and look at the underlined word or words. Choose the word or phrase that means about the same thing as the underlined word or phrase. Mark the correct answer.

1. Anything that has <u>not yet happened</u> is in the ...
- ○ household
- ● future
- ○ dungeon

2. Something <u>far away</u> is in the ...
- ○ century
- ○ coolness
- ● distance

3. The <u>person who writes</u> a paper or a book is the ...
- ○ disease
- ○ hamster
- ● author

4. To <u>walk through shallow water</u> is to ...
- ○ haul
- ○ shatter
- ● wade

5. To <u>talk in front of other people</u> is to give a ...
- ○ shriek
- ○ savage
- ● speech

6. A <u>large meal</u> is a ...
- ○ freckle
- ○ drill
- ● feast

7. A <u>person in a story</u> is a ...
- ● character
- ○ clump
- ○ seller

8. <u>How much a person or thing weighs</u> is his ...
- ○ intend
- ○ freight
- ● weight

9. When you <u>offer an idea</u>, you give a ...
- ○ prop
- ○ major
- ● suggestion

10. A <u>puzzling question or problem</u> is a ...
- ● riddle
- ○ valve
- ○ wrestler

©Kelley Wingate CD 3735   54

Name _____

Skill: Grammar and Punctuation

DIRECTIONS:
Read each sentence and look at the underlined word or words. If there is no error in capitalization or punctuation, mark the answer "correct." If there is an error, choose the answer that has the correct capitalization and punctuation.

1. Susan lives in <u>new york</u>.
- ○ correct
- ● New York
- ○ New york
- ○ new York

2. <u>What did the mailman</u> bring to the door?
- ○ correct
- ○ what did the Mailman
- ○ What did the Mailman
- ● What did the mailman

3. Kelly will <u>sing and,</u> Peggy will dance.
- ○ correct
- ● sing, and
- ○ sing; and
- ○ sing. and

4. It is almost dark. <u>we'd better hurry</u> home!
- ○ correct
- ○ W'ed better hurry
- ○ We'd Better hurry
- ● We'd better hurry

5. My favorite book is called <u>The silver peach.</u>
- ○ correct
- ● The Silver Peach
- ○ the Silver Peach
- ○ the silver peach

6. What a surprise! How did you know it was just what I <u>wanted.</u>
- ○ correct
- ○ wanted,
- ● wanted?
- ○ Wanted.

7. I used <u>red, green, and yellow</u> dots on my monster.
- ● correct
- ○ red green, and yellow
- ○ red, green, and, yellow
- ○ red, green and yellow,

8. <u>Kevin's aunt</u> is coming to visit next week.
- ● correct
- ○ Kevins' aunt
- ○ Kevins's aunt
- ○ Kevins Aunt

9. Jeff lives in <u>Detroit Michigan</u>.
- ○ correct
- ○ Detroit, michigan
- ● Detroit, Michigan
- ○ detroit, michigan

10. Is today the day of <u>our picnic?</u>
- ● correct
- ○ our Picnic?
- ○ our picnic!
- ○ our picnic.

©Kelley Wingate CD 3735   55

Name _____

Skill: Grammar and Punctuation

DIRECTIONS:
Read each sentence and look at the underlined word or words. If there is no error in capitalization or punctuation, mark the answer "correct." If there is an error, choose the answer that has the correct capitalization and punctuation.

1. <u>when will we be</u> leaving for the airport?
- ○ correct
- ○ when will we, be
- ○ When will, we be
- ● When will we be

2. <u>kevins dog</u> dug a huge hole under the fence!
- ○ correct
- ○ Kevins dog
- ○ kevin's dog
- ● Kevin's dog

3. I went to <u>Washington, DC</u> with my parents.
- ○ correct
- ○ washington, d.c.
- ○ Washington D.C.
- ● Washington, D.C.

4. <u>Fran and Billy</u> were surprised to see me at the party!
- ● correct
- ○ Fran, and billy
- ○ Fran and Billy,
- ○ Fran and billy

5. My older brother goes to <u>woodlake middle school</u>.
- ○ correct
- ○ Woodlake middle school
- ● Woodlake Middle School
- ○ Woodlake Middle, School

6. Peter asked <u>Mr Smith</u> to come to our school play.
- ○ correct
- ● Mr. Smith
- ○ mr. Smith
- ○ Mr smith

7. Jay has a pet <u>parrot. And a</u> small brown rabbit.
- ○ correct
- ● parrot and a
- ○ parrot! And a
- ○ parrot and, a

8. I put the <u>ornaments, lights, and star</u> on the tree.
- ● correct
- ○ ornaments lights, and star
- ○ ornaments lights and star
- ○ ornaments, lights, and , star

9. It is time to go. <u>let's hurry, or we</u> will miss the train!
- ○ correct
- ○ Let's hurry or We
- ● Let's hurry, or we
- ○ Let's, hurry or we

10. It looks like rain. Shall we take our umbrellas <u>to the park.</u>
- ○ correct
- ○ to the Park.
- ○ to the park!
- ● to the park?

©Kelley Wingate CD 3735   56

Answer Key

Name _____

Skill: Grammar and Punctuation

DIRECTIONS:
Read each sentence and look at the underlined word or words. If there is no error in capitalization or punctuation, mark the answer "correct." If there is an error, choose the answer that has the correct capitalization and punctuation.

1. Will you <u>come with us. I think</u> you will enjoy the journey.
   - ○ correct
   - ○ come with us, I think
   - ● come with us? I think
   - ○ come with us? i think

2. <u>Jack's parents</u> took a three week trip to China last year.
   - ● correct
   - ○ Jacks parents
   - ○ jack's parents
   - ○ Jack's Parents

3. <u>put the camera on</u> the top shelf so it won't get broken!
   - ○ correct
   - ○ Put the Camera on
   - ● Put the camera on
   - ○ Put the camera. On

4. Are they here <u>yet? I would like to</u> meet them.
   - ● correct
   - ○ yet, I would like to
   - ○ yet. I would like to
   - ○ yet! I would, like to

5. Have you ever read the book called <u>come home tomorrow</u>?
   - ○ correct
   - ○ come home tomorrow !
   - ○ Come home tomorrow ?
   - ● Come Home Tomorrow ?

6. Ben lives on <u>hartman street</u>, near the bus stop.
   - ○ correct
   - ○ hartman Street
   - ○ Hartman street
   - ● Hartman Street

7. <u>Betty, Jane, Cora and Patty</u> are coming to my party.
   - ○ correct
   - ● Betty, Jane, Cora, and Patty
   - ○ Betty Jane, Cora and Patty
   - ○ Betty, Jane, Cora, and Patty,

8. <u>Havent</u> you finished your homework yet?
   - ○ correct
   - ○ havent
   - ○ Have'nt
   - ● Haven't

9. <u>That Dinosaur is</u> my favorite one in the museum!
   - ○ correct
   - ● That dinosaur is
   - ○ That Dinosaur, is
   - ○ That dinosaur. Is

10. <u>Miss silbert is a very</u> good teacher.
    - ○ correct
    - ● Miss Silbert is a very
    - ○ Miss silbert, is a very
    - ○ Miss Silbert, is a very

©Kelley Wingate CD 3735 — 57

Name _____

Skill: Capitalization and Punctuation—Test 4

DIRECTIONS:
Read each sentence and look at the underlined word or words. If there is no error in capitalization or punctuation, mark the answer "correct." If there is an error, choose the answer that has the correct capitalization and punctuation.

1. There were <u>six student's</u> in the room after lunch.
   - ○ correct
   - ○ six Student's
   - ● six students
   - ○ six students'

2. <u>I did'nt know</u> that Jason and Steve are brothers!
   - ○ correct
   - ○ i didn't know
   - ○ I didnt know
   - ● I didn't know

3. <u>Alice marie is</u> my best friend.
   - ○ correct
   - ● Alice Marie is
   - ○ Alice, Marie is
   - ○ Alice, Marie, is

4. What time <u>is it? I</u> can't see the clock from here.
   - ● correct
   - ○ is it, I
   - ○ is it! I
   - ○ is it? i

5. The bird is in <u>her nest. I think</u> she has some eggs in there.
   - ○ correct
   - ● her nest. I think
   - ○ her nest; i think
   - ○ her nest? I think

6. Did you know that <u>tomorrow is my tenth birthday!</u>
   - ○ correct
   - ○ tomorrow is my tenth birthday.
   - ○ tomorrow, is my tenth Birthday!
   - ● tomorrow is my tenth birthday?

7. Ken will set the <u>table and</u> wash the dishes.
   - ● correct
   - ○ table, and
   - ○ table and,
   - ○ table: and

8. <u>Joe, Tom, and Bill</u> want to play soccer after school.
   - ● correct
   - ○ Joe, tom, and bill
   - ○ Joe, Tom and Bill
   - ○ Joe Tom and Bill

9. Nancy has a cousin that lives in <u>Peidmont Oregon.</u>
   - ○ correct
   - ○ peidmont oregon.
   - ○ Peidmont Oregon;
   - ● Peidmont, Oregon.

10. <u>Elly and craig</u> are building a club house today!
    - ○ correct
    - ○ elly and craig
    - ○ elly and Craig
    - ● Elly and Craig

© Carson-Dellosa CD-3735 — 58

Name _____

Skill: Capitalization and Punctuation—Test 5

DIRECTIONS:
Read each sentence and look at the underlined word or words. If there is no error in capitalization or punctuation, mark the answer "correct." If there is an error, choose the answer that has the correct capitalization and punctuation.

1. I will have <u>pizza potato chips and cola</u> for lunch!
   - ○ correct
   - ○ pizza, potato, chips and cola
   - ● pizza, potato chips, and cola
   - ○ pizza, potato, chips and cola,

2. Which dress do you think I should wear <u>to the dance?</u>
   - ● correct
   - ○ to the Dance?
   - ○ to the dance!
   - ○ to the dance.

3. <u>This dictionary has</u> two words that are not spelled correctly!
   - ● correct
   - ○ This Dictionary has
   - ○ This Dictionary, has
   - ○ This dictionary, has

4. I stood on the <u>golden gate bridge</u> in San Francisco!
   - ○ correct
   - ● Golden Gate Bridge
   - ○ Golden Gate bridge
   - ○ Golden gate bridge

5. I don't like that <u>movie. Because it</u> frightens me too much!
   - ○ correct
   - ● movie because it
   - ○ movie because, it
   - ○ Movie. Because it

6. <u>Main street is</u> usually in the center of a town or city.
   - ○ correct
   - ○ Main street are
   - ● Main Street is
   - ○ Main Street are

7. <u>use glue, glitter, and silver</u> paint to make this beautiful picture frame.
   - ○ correct
   - ○ Use glue glitter and silver
   - ○ Use glue, glitter and, silver
   - ● Use glue, glitter, and silver

8. Martha had a small <u>part in the play.</u>
   - ● correct
   - ○ part in the Play.
   - ○ part in the play?
   - ○ part, in the play.

9. Cindy said that <u>Mindys letter</u> arrived in the mail today!
   - ○ correct
   - ○ Mindys Letter
   - ● Mindy's letter
   - ○ mindys' letter

10. Do you think <u>your new Neighbor</u> has moved in yet?
    - ○ correct
    - ○ Your new Neighbor
    - ○ your new, neighbor
    - ● your new neighbor

© Carson-Dellosa CD-3735 — 59

Name _____

Skill: Grammar and Punctuation

DIRECTIONS:
Read each sentence and look at the underlined word or words. If there is no error in capitalization or punctuation, mark the answer "correct." If there is an error, choose the answer that has the correct capitalization and punctuation.

1. The prettiest flowers are <u>Roses and Tulips.</u>
   - ○ correct
   - ○ Roses and Tulips?
   - ● roses and tulips.
   - ○ Roses and Tulips!

2. <u>Meg and Tony hid</u> the treasure behind the stone wall.
   - ● correct
   - ○ Meg, and Tony
   - ○ Meg, and tony
   - ○ meg, and tony

3. <u>Miss Snows third grade class</u> won the tug-of-war contest!
   - ○ correct
   - ○ Miss Snow's Third grade class
   - ○ Miss Snows Third Grade class
   - ● Miss Snow's third grade class

4. Is that you under that <u>mask! I</u> couldn't tell who it was!
   - ○ correct
   - ○ Mask! I
   - ○ mask, I
   - ● mask? I

5. Did you hear <u>what I just said!</u>
   - ○ correct
   - ○ what i just said!
   - ○ what I just said.
   - ● what I just said?

6. <u>Harry and David is</u> my friends.
   - ○ correct
   - ○ Harry and david is
   - ○ Harry and david are
   - ● Harry and David are

7. Do you live on <u>Elm street or Oak street?</u>
   - ○ correct
   - ○ Elm street or Oak street.
   - ● Elm Street or Oak Street?
   - ○ Elm Street or Oak Street,

8. We had <u>roast turkey and stuffing</u> for dinner last night.
   - ○ correct
   - ○ roast turkey, and stuffing
   - ○ roast Turkey and stuffing
   - ○ Roast Turkey, and stuffing

9. We went to <u>Disney world for our</u> vacation last year.
   - ○ correct
   - ○ disney world for Our
   - ○ Disney World for Our
   - ● Disney World for our

10. I asked <u>Amy, Susie, and Bonnie,</u> to come to my house today.
    - ○ correct
    - ○ Amy Susie and Bonnie.
    - ● Amy, Susie, and Bonnie.
    - ○ Amy, Susie, and Bonnie,

©Kelley Wingate CD 3735 — 60

©Kelley Wingate CD 3735 — 119

Answer Key

Name _____

Skill: Capitalization and Punctuation—Test 7

DIRECTIONS:
Read each sentence and look at the underlined word or words. If there is no error in capitalization or punctuation, mark the answer "correct." If there is an error, choose the answer that has the correct capitalization and punctuation.

1. Greenleaf ave is the longest street in town.
   - ○ correct
   - ● Greenleaf Ave.
   - ○ Greenleaf ave.
   - ○ greenleaf ave.

2. I will be careful crossing the street.
   - ● correct
   - ○ crossing the Street!
   - ○ crossing the Street?
   - ○ crossing the street?

3. It is a windy day in april. I think I will fly a kite!
   - ○ correct
   - ○ day. In april I think
   - ● day in April. I think
   - ○ day in April I think

4. The young robin flew across the sky.
   - ● correct
   - ○ young Robin flew
   - ○ young, robin flew
   - ○ young robin. Flew

5. It is cold outside all the trees are bare.
   - ○ correct
   - ● outside. All
   - ○ outside, all
   - ○ Outside. All

6. we have a new television!
   - ○ correct
   - ○ We Have
   - ○ we Have
   - ● We have

7. Mom likes to cook she cooks great dinners!
   - ○ correct
   - ○ to. Cook she cooks great.
   - ● to cook. She cooks great
   - ○ to cook she. Cooks great

8. My grandmothers picture is on the table in my bedroom.
   - ○ correct
   - ○ Grandmothers
   - ● grandmother's
   - ○ Grandmothers'

9. The circus tent is red, and yellow with blue stripes.
   - ○ correct
   - ○ red and yellow, with blue,
   - ○ red, and yellow, with blue
   - ● red and yellow with blue

10. Last friday was the first day of October.
   - ○ correct
   - ○ friday, was
   - ○ Friday Was
   - ● Friday was

Name _____

Skill: Capitalization and Punctuation—Test 8

DIRECTIONS:
Read each sentence and look at the underlined word or words. If there is no error in capitalization or punctuation, mark the answer "correct." If there is an error, choose the answer that has the correct capitalization and punctuation.

1. When will you go to california.
   - ○ correct
   - ● go to California?
   - ○ go to california.
   - ○ go to california?

2. The mice did not hear the cat's bell in time!
   - ● correct
   - ○ cats bell
   - ○ Cat's Bell
   - ○ Cats bell

3. Jim painted a picture of leave's and flower's.
   - ○ correct
   - ○ leave and flower
   - ○ leaves and flowers'
   - ● leaves and flowers

4. I have a lot of fun when I stay with aunt Phyllis.
   - ○ correct
   - ○ aunt phyllis
   - ○ Aunt phyllis
   - ● Aunt Phyllis

5. I have a red car, chris has a blue car.
   - ○ correct
   - ○ car. chris
   - ○ Car. Chris
   - ● car. Chris

6. Joe Tom and Frank are in my class.
   - ○ correct
   - ○ Joe, tom, and frank
   - ● Joe, Tom, and Frank
   - ○ Joe Tom, and Frank

7. My brother and Sister went to the store with our neighbor.
   - ○ correct
   - ● brother and sister
   - ○ Brother and Sister
   - ○ brother, and sister

8. The school bus slipped on the muddy road.
   - ● correct
   - ○ The School bus
   - ○ The School Bus
   - ○ The school Bus

9. The bird's made a nest in the top of that tree.
   - ○ correct
   - ● birds made a nest
   - ○ birds' made a nest
   - ○ Birds made a nest

10. Did that elephant just eat a peanut?
   - ● correct
   - ○ just eat a peanut!
   - ○ just eat. a peanut?
   - ○ just eat a peanut.

Name _____

Skill: Capitalization and Punctuation—Test 9

DIRECTIONS:
Read each sentence and look at the underlined word or words. If there is no error in capitalization or punctuation, mark the answer "correct." If there is an error, choose the answer that has the correct capitalization and punctuation.

1. many people like to dance when the music plays.
   - ○ correct
   - ○ Many People like
   - ○ Many people. Like
   - ● Many people like

2. We walked, and walked for many miles.
   - ○ correct
   - ○ walked, and walked,
   - ● walked and walked
   - ○ walked: and walked

3. My Horse and Monkey are good friends!
   - ○ correct
   - ● horse and monkey
   - ○ Horse, and monkey
   - ○ horse and monkey,

4. James would like to play in the school band.
   - ○ correct
   - ○ School Band.
   - ○ School band.
   - ● school band.

5. Judy just read The Wind in the Willows.
   - ● correct
   - ○ the Wind In The Willows
   - ○ The Wind In The Willows
   - ○ the Wind in The willows

6. The whale is one of the largest Animals in the world.
   - ○ correct
   - ○ Largest Animals
   - ○ largest animal
   - ● largest animals

7. Mr. Klein is one of the nicest men I know!
   - ● correct
   - ○ mr klein
   - ○ Mr. klein
   - ○ Mr. Klein.

8. The train had an engine six cars and a caboose!
   - ○ correct
   - ○ Engine six cars and a
   - ○ engine, six cars and a,
   - ● engine, six cars, and a

9. Have you ever seen the empire state building in New York?
   - ○ correct
   - ○ Empire state building
   - ● Empire State Building
   - ○ Empire state Building

10. Wendys shoes were covered in mud after the storm.
   - ○ correct
   - ● Wendy's shoes
   - ○ Wendys' shoes
   - ○ Wendys shoe's

Name _____

Skill: Capitalization and Punctuation—Test 10

DIRECTIONS:
Read each sentence and look at the underlined word or words. If there is no error in capitalization or punctuation, mark the answer "correct." If there is an error, choose the answer that has the correct capitalization and punctuation.

1. My uncle lives in Tampa Florida.
   - ○ correct
   - ● Tampa, Florida
   - ○ tampa florida
   - ○ Tampa; Florida

2. The paper and paints' are ready for art class.
   - ○ correct
   - ○ Paper and Paints
   - ● paper and paints
   - ○ paper and paint's

3. Mother and father is a very good movie.
   - ○ correct
   - ○ Mother And Father
   - ● Mother and Father
   - ○ mother and Father

4. Will it rain? or will it snow?
   - ○ correct
   - ○ Rain? Or will
   - ○ rain! Or will
   - ● rain? Or will

5. Did you see the ending of the race? Who won?
   - ● correct
   - ○ race! Who won!
   - ○ race! Who won?
   - ○ race. Who won?

6. Vera chose silver, blue red, and green as her four colors.
   - ○ correct
   - ○ silver blue, red, and green
   - ● silver, blue, red, and green
   - ○ silver, blue, red, and, green

7. Juan's sister is only three years old.
   - ● correct
   - ○ Juans sister
   - ○ Juans Sister
   - ○ Juans' sister

8. Terry and i are planning a picnic for next Saturday.
   - ○ correct
   - ○ terry and I
   - ● Terry and I
   - ○ terry and i

9. This letter is addressed to Dr. Paul J Keller.
   - ○ correct
   - ○ Dr. Paul. J Keller
   - ○ Dr Paul. J. Keller
   - ● Dr. Paul J. Keller

10. George will meet you on the steps of the library next saturday morning.
   - ○ correct
   - ● library next Saturday morning
   - ○ Library next Saturday morning
   - ○ library next Saturday Morning

Answer Key

Name _____

Skill: Narrative Passages

DIRECTIONS:
Read each story, then read each question. Read all the answers, then mark the space for the answer you think is right. Mark NH (not here) if the answer can't be figured out from the given information.

Sarah took the scissors and tape from the desk. She chose a roll of blue wrapping paper with silver stars on it. She slipped into her brother's room and took his crayons and glue. Sarah quietly went to her room and closed the door. Sarah took a large box from her closet. It was a model ship for Danny's birthday. Sarah had saved her money for three weeks to buy this present. She knew Danny would like it. He had lots of models, but none like this! Sarah wrapped the box and hid it in the closet.

1. Where did Sarah find the glue and crayons?
   ○ in the desk
   ○ in her room
   ● in her brother's room
   ○ NH

2. What color was the wrapping paper?
   ○ green with red hearts
   ● blue with silver stars
   ○ silver with blue stars
   ○ NH

3. Why was Sarah being so quiet?
   ○ she didn't feel well
   ○ she was hiding
   ● she wanted to surprise Danny
   ○ NH

4. How did Sarah know that Danny would like her present?
   ○ she likes Danny
   ● Danny likes models
   ○ Danny likes crayons and glue
   ○ NH

5. What is the name of Sarah's brother?
   ○ Mark
   ○ Danny
   ○ Frank
   ● NH

6. When will it be Danny's birthday?
   ○ today
   ○ June 3
   ○ in three weeks
   ● NH

7. Why did Sarah hide the present after she had wrapped it?
   ● it is a surprise
   ○ she didn't like how it looked
   ○ Sarah wanted the model herself
   ○ NH

8. What words from the story help you know that Sarah is trying to keep a secret?
   ○ scissors, crayons, closed
   ○ saved, models, wrapped
   ● slipped, quietly, hid
   ○ NH

© Carson-Dellosa CD-3735   65

Name _____

Skill: Narrative Passages

DIRECTIONS:
Read each story, then read each question. Read all the answers, then mark the space for the answer you think is right. Mark NH (not here) if the answer can't be figured out from the given information.

Kerry poured water into the bottle and added ice, then screwed the lid on tightly. He did not want the bottle to leak on this trip! He opened a large paper bag and put the water bottle inside. Kerry made four peanut butter sandwiches and wrapped them carefully. Would a jar of pickles travel well? Kerry decided they would not. Instead, he found a bag of chips and tossed them into the bag. Three bananas, two apples, and some carrots were added. Oops! He almost forgot the cookies!

1. What was the first item Kerry put in the paper bag?
   ○ cookies
   ○ sandwiches
   ● water bottle
   ○ NH

2. What was Kerry doing?
   ● packing food for a trip
   ○ fixing his breakfast
   ○ making dinner
   ○ NH

3. Where was Kerry going?
   ○ to his friend's house
   ○ on a picnic
   ○ on a bike trip
   ● NH

4. How many fruits did Kerry put into the bag?
   ○ 4
   ● 5
   ○ 6
   ○ NH

5. Why did Kerry add ice to the bottle of water?
   ○ to make more water
   ● to cool the water
   ○ to keep the food cool
   ○ NH

6. Why did Kerry decide not to take the pickles?
   ○ he doesn't like pickles
   ● the jar might break
   ○ the pickles were too sour
   ○ NH

7. How old is Kerry?
   ○ 10
   ○ 13
   ○ 17
   ● NH

8. Which of these places would Kerry probably not be going?
   ○ on a picnic
   ● to a restaurant
   ○ to the beach
   ○ NH

© Carson-Dellosa CD-3735   66

Name _____

Skill: Narrative Passages

DIRECTIONS:
Read each story, then read each question. Read all the answers, then mark the space for the answer you think is right. Mark NH (not here) if the answer can't be figured out from the given information.

It was the morning of the school spelling bee. Greg's stomach was in knots. Had he studied well enough? Would he look foolish in front of everyone? Greg stood on the stage with the other children. As the teacher went through the group, Greg spelled his words correctly. Soon there were only two students left, Greg and Polly! The teacher asked Polly to spell "nervous." Polly spelled it the wrong way. Greg looked at the teacher and began to grin. He knew he could spell that word!

1. Who is the main character in this story?
   ● Greg
   ○ Polly
   ○ the teacher
   ○ NH

2. Why was Greg's stomach in knots?
   ○ he had a cold
   ○ he didn't want to go to school
   ● he was nervous
   ○ NH

3. What was the name of Polly and Greg's school?
   ○ Keller Elementary School
   ○ Woodlake Middle School
   ○ Bradshaw School
   ● NH

4. How many children were in the spelling bee when it started?
   ○ a lot
   ○ twenty-five
   ○ two
   ● NH

5. What word did Polly misspell?
   ○ encyclopedia
   ● nervous
   ○ a hard word
   ○ NH

6. What word would best describe Greg's feelings at the beginning of the contest?
   ● worried
   ○ excited
   ○ calm
   ○ NH

7. Why did Greg grin at the teacher at the end of the story?
   ○ Polly had missed the word
   ● Greg knew he could win
   ○ He liked the teacher
   ○ NH

8. What had Greg done to prepare for the spelling bee?
   ○ combed his hair
   ● studied the words
   ○ acted foolish for his friends
   ○ NH

© Carson-Dellosa CD-3735   67

Name _____

Skill: Narrative Passages

DIRECTIONS:
Read each story, then read each question. Read all the answers, then mark the space for the answer you think is right. Mark NH (not here) if the answer can't be figured out from the given information.

Beth and Erin wanted to surprise their mother with breakfast in bed. They got up early and raced to the kitchen. Beth measured flour and milk while Erin mixed in the eggs and spices. The girls heated a large flat pan and poured out four perfect pancakes. When the tops were bubbled, Beth carefully flipped them over. Beth fixed a tray with a glass of orange juice and a fork. Erin put the finished pancakes on a plate and slid it onto the tray. Breakfast looked wonderful, but the kitchen was a mess!

1. What are the names of the girls in this story?
   ○ Beth and Mother
   ● Erin and Beth
   ○ Beth and Evan
   ○ NH

2. What were the girls making for breakfast?
   ○ eggs and juice
   ○ eggs and pancakes
   ● pancakes and juice
   ○ NH

3. Why were the two girls making breakfast?
   ● to surprise mother
   ○ they were hungry
   ○ for a girl scout badge
   ○ NH

4. How did they know when to turn the pancake?
   ○ the bottom was done
   ● the top was bubbly
   ○ the pancakes started to smoke
   ○ NH

5. Why were the girls trying to surprise their mother?
   ○ it was her birthday
   ○ it was Mother's Day
   ○ Mother had been working hard
   ● NH

6. How many pancakes did the girls make?
   ○ 2
   ● 4
   ○ 6
   ○ NH

7. What was on the finished tray?
   ○ juice, pancakes, fork
   ○ fork, plate, juice, flower
   ● plate, pancakes, juice, fork
   ○ NH

8. What relationship do the girls share?
   ● they are sisters
   ○ they are cousins
   ○ they are friends
   ○ NH

© Carson-Dellosa CD-3735   68

Answer Key

DIRECTIONS:
Read each story, then read each question. Read all the answers, then mark the space for the answer you think is right. Mark NH (not here) if the answer can't be figured out from the given information.

Troop 347 was camping. The tents were set up and all the girls were having a lot of fun. Everyone but Elly, that is. Elly was a little worried. She had never stayed out overnight without her parents. She was afraid she might get homesick and cry. All the other girls would laugh and tease her. That night the girls crawled into their sleeping bags and giggled in the dark. Elly didn't know what to do. She was scared. She closed her eyes and thought about her own room with her parents next door. Before she knew it, Elly was asleep!

1. What was the number of Elly's scout troop?
- ● 347
- ○ 437
- ○ 743
- ○ NH

2. Where were the scouts sleeping?
- ○ in cabins
- ○ under the stars
- ● in tents
- ○ NH

3. What was Elly's problem?
- ○ she hated camping
- ○ she didn't have any friends
- ● she was homesick
- ○ NH

4. Which words from the story best tell how Elly is feeling?
- ○ camping, tease, parents
- ● worried, scared, afraid
- ○ dark, overnight, crawled
- ○ NH

5. How did Elly solve her problem?
- ● she pretended to be home
- ○ she told the troop leader
- ○ she stayed awake all night
- ○ NH

6. Where did the troop go camping?
- ○ in the mountains
- ○ in the forest
- ○ by the ocean
- ● NH

7. How did the other girls feel about the camping trip?
- ○ they were scared, too
- ○ they wanted to go home
- ● they were having a good time
- ○ NH

8. How many girls were in Elly's tent when they went to bed?
- ○ four
- ○ seven
- ○ ten
- ● NH

DIRECTIONS:
Read each story, then read each question. Read all the answers, then mark the space for the answer you think is right. Mark NH (not here) if the answer can't be figured out from the given information.

The city lay spread out beneath the plane as Bob looked out the window of the airplane. The Statue of Liberty stood with her arm raised high in the sky. Bob was very excited. This was his first trip to the city, and there were many things he wanted to do. His family had tickets to a Broadway play for that evening. Bob had read about the city and knew just what he wanted to see. He was going to the Empire State Building because it was one of the tallest skyscrapers. He also wanted to take a carriage ride through Central Park.

1. Who is Bob going to be with while he visits this city?
- ○ his uncle
- ○ his friend
- ● his family
- ○ NH

2. What city is Bob coming to visit?
- ○ Chicago
- ● New York
- ○ San Francisco
- ○ NH

3. Why is Bob so excited?
- ● there are so many things to see
- ○ he has never flown before
- ○ he is coming to a new country
- ○ NH

4. What words in the story help you know which city Bob is going to visit?
- ● Statue of Liberty, Broadway
- ○ skyscrapers, carriage
- ○ plane, city
- ○ NH

5. What will Bob go see first when the plane lands?
- ○ Empire State Building
- ○ Statue of Liberty
- ○ a Broadway play
- ● NH

6. Where does Bob live?
- ○ Central Park
- ○ New York
- ○ San Francisco
- ● NH

7. Where does Bob want to go to ride in a carriage?
- ○ Statue of Liberty
- ● Central Park
- ○ Broadway
- ○ NH

8. What word best tells how Bob is feeling as he flies over this city?
- ○ fierce
- ○ angry
- ● cheerful
- ○ NH

DIRECTIONS:
Read each story, then read each question. Read all the answers, then mark the space for the answer you think is right. Mark NH (not here) if the answer can't be figured out from the given information.

My grandpa is one of the nicest people I know. He lives far away, but I see him many times each year. My Grandpa calls me twice a week, and we talk for a long time! When grandpa comes to visit, we take walks by the river. We go to the movies and fly kites. Grandpa showed me how to make a model airplane out of toothpicks and tissue paper. He is always ready to play baseball or soccer whenever I want. He is never too busy to listen to me. I think he is the best grandpa anyone ever had!

1. Who is this story about?
- ○ my father
- ● my grandfather
- ○ me
- ○ NH

2. How many times does Grandpa visit me each year?
- ○ twice
- ○ four times
- ● many times
- ○ NH

3. Where does my grandpa live?
- ● far away
- ○ next door
- ○ in the next state
- ○ NH

4. What words do I use in this story to describe my grandpa?
- ○ baseball and models
- ● best and nicest
- ○ twice and visit
- ○ NH

5. Who is telling this story?
- ○ a niece
- ○ a grandson
- ○ a granddaughter
- ● NH

6. What word best describes my time with Grandpa?
- ○ unfair
- ○ dreadful
- ● pleasant
- ○ NH

7. What is something Grandpa would never do with me?
- ○ go bowling
- ○ ride bikes
- ○ play a game
- ● NH

8. How do you think Grandpa feels when he comes to visit me?
- ○ disappointed
- ○ stubborn
- ● merry
- ○ NH

DIRECTIONS:
Read each story, then read each question. Read all the answers, then mark the space for the answer you think is right. Mark NH (not here) if the answer can't be figured out from the given information.

Lucy sat down at the computer and began to write a letter to her pen pal, Jenny. Lucy wrote about the project she was doing in school. Her class had collected a lot of stones and was sorting them by color and shape. They were going to find out about each stone and write reports about them. Lucy knew that Jenny lived near the mountains. She wanted Jenny to find a stone and mail it to her. Lucy was sure that the class would be surprised at the unusual stone she would bring in!

1. Who is Jenny?
- ○ Lucy's cousin
- ● Lucy's pen pal
- ○ Lucy's aunt
- ○ NH

2. What did Lucy write about in her letter to Jenny?
- ○ stones
- ● the class project
- ○ mountains
- ○ NH

3. What kind of stone did Lucy want Jenny to send?
- ○ a very large stone
- ○ a red stone
- ● different from what she has
- ○ NH

4. Why did Lucy want Jenny to send a stone?
- ● to surprise the class
- ○ to look for gold
- ○ to add to Lucy's rock collection
- ○ NH

5. How did Lucy and Jenny become pen pals?
- ○ they looked for stones together
- ○ they met at the beach
- ○ they were good friends
- ● NH

6. Where does Jenny live?
- ● near mountains
- ○ near the ocean
- ○ near a big river
- ○ NH

7. What will the class do with the stones?
- ○ display them for the school
- ● find out what kind they are
- ○ mail them to Jenny
- ○ NH

8. What word might best describe Lucy's class when they see the unusual stone?
- ○ thirsty
- ○ ashamed
- ● curious
- ○ NH

Answer Key

Name _____

Skill: Narrative Passages

DIRECTIONS:
Read each story, then read each question. Read all the answers, then mark the space for the answer you think is right. Mark NH (not here) if the answer can't be figured out from the given information.

Dan felt the car begin to shake as if he were driving over rocks. The road looked smooth. He slowed down and pulled over to the edge of the road. Dan got out of the car and walked to the back. The back tire on the passenger side was flat! Dan was already late and didn't need this problem. He opened the trunk and took out the jack. Before long, he was ready to replace the flat tire. Dan looked in the trunk to find the spare tire. As he took it out, he noticed that the spare tire was flat, too! Now what was he going to do?

1. What would be a good name for this story?
○ Dan
○ How to Change a Flat Tire
● Dan and the Flat Tire
○ NH

2. Where was Dan when he got the flat tire?
○ in the city
○ in the country
○ in a park
● NH

3. What did Dan take from the trunk first?
○ the spare tire
● a jack
○ his jacket
○ NH

4. How did Dan know something was wrong with the car?
● he could feel it shaking
○ he could hear it banging
○ he saw the glass he ran over
○ NH

5. Why was Dan unhappy about the flat tire?
○ he didn't have a spare
● he was already late
○ he wasn't unhappy
○ NH

6. How did Dan get a flat tire?
○ it was old and just wore out
○ he ran over some glass
○ he ran over some nails
● NH

7. What word would best describe how Dan is feeling at the end of the story?
○ powerful
● hopeless
○ content
○ NH

8. What would be a good thing for Dan to do now?
○ find a phone and get help
○ drive on the flat tire
○ wait until someone misses him
● NH

© Carson-Dellosa CD-3735

73

Name _____

Skill: Narrative Passages

DIRECTIONS:
Read each story, then read each question. Read all the answers, then mark the space for the answer you think is right. Mark NH (not here) if the answer can't be figured out from the given information.

Mike and Joe were sitting in front of the television. It was Friday and Joe was spending the night at Mike's house. They planned on staying up all night! They watched a movie, then made some popcorn. Joe got out the checkers and the boys played three games. Mike turned out the lights and they made silly shadows on the wall with their flashlights. The boys began to yawn, but they told each other they were not tired. Mike looked at the clock. It was only eleven o'clock. What a long night!

1. In who's house were the boys spending the night?
○ Joe's
● Mike's
○ Mike and Joe's
○ NH

2. What did the boys do first?
● watch a movie
○ play checkers
○ eat popcorn
○ NH

3. Why did the boys begin to yawn?
○ they were bored
● they were tired
○ it was warm in the room
○ NH

4. How many games of checkers did the boys play?
○ two
● three
○ four
○ NH

5. How old are the boys?
○ eight
○ nine
○ ten
● NH

6. How did the boys feel at the beginning of the story?
○ terrible
● excited
○ lonely
○ NH

7. How did the boys feel at the end of the story?
○ wide awake
○ important
● tired
○ NH

8. What did the boys do after eleven o'clock?
○ watch television
○ eat more popcorn
○ play a game
● NH

© Carson-Dellosa CD-3735

74

Name _____

Skill: Narrative Passages

DIRECTIONS:
Read each story, then read each question. Read all the answers, then mark the space for the answer you think is right. Mark NH (not here) if the answer can't be figured out from the given information.

Casey's mom was having a garage sale. She had one last year, too, so Casey was not surprised to see her old clothes and toys in the boxes. Many people had come to the house and were looking at the things spread on the driveway. Suddenly Casey saw her favorite bear in one of the boxes. A little boy was just picking it up. He asked his mom if he could have it. Casey wanted to cry. She had not wanted her bear to be in the sale! The boy's mother was handing him some money.

1. What would be a good title for this story?
○ Casey's Bear
● The Garage Sale Mistake
○ A Sale
○ NH

2. Who is the main character in this story?
○ the boy
○ Casey's mom
● Casey
○ NH

3. How did Casey feel when she saw that the boy wanted her bear?
● upset
○ worried
○ angry
○ NH

4. Who put the bear in the garage sale?
○ Casey
○ Casey's mom
○ the boy
● NH

5. Why did the mother hand money to the boy?
○ it was his money
○ she wanted him to hold it
● to buy the bear
○ NH

6. How did Casey learn about garage sales?
● they had one last year
○ she had been to many of them
○ she read about them
○ NH

7. Who came to the garage sale?
○ neighbors
○ friends
○ no one
● NH

8. Which sentence best describes how Casey feels about her bear?
○ Casey thinks the bear is smart.
○ Casey wants to sell the bear.
● Casey loves the bear.
○ NH

© Carson-Dellosa CD-3735

75

Name _____

Skill: Narrative Passages

DIRECTIONS:
Read each story, then read each question. Read all the answers, then mark the space for the answer you think is right. Mark NH (not here) if the answer can't be figured out from the given information.

My favorite place in the world is the beach. I like to hear the waves as they roar onto the shore. The wind blows a little of the spray in my face if I sit close enough. Sometimes I like to lay in the sand close to the water. The waves lift my legs, and they float a little before the water slips away. There is nothing better than to feel the warm sun on my back and the cool water on my feet! I like to build sand castles, too. Once I made one that was over five feet tall!

1. Who is telling this story?
○ a boy
○ a girl
○ an adult
● NH

2. Where is my favorite place?
○ in the sand
○ in the water
● at the beach
○ NH

3. What does the wind blow into my face?
○ sand
● water
○ sun
○ NH

4. How tall was the castle I once made?
● five feet
○ six feet
○ seven feet
○ NH

5. What is a good title for this story?
○ Sunny Days
○ Building Sand Castles
● My Favorite Place
○ NH

6. What don't I talk about doing at the beach?
○ cooling my feet
○ building castles
● swimming
○ NH

7. Which is my favorite thing to do at the beach?
○ float on the waves
○ build sand castles
● feel the warm sun
○ NH

8. What words might describe how I feel when I am at the beach?
○ weak
● wonderful
○ wealthy
○ NH

© Carson-Dellosa CD-3735

76

Answer Key

Name _____

Skill: Expository Passages

DIRECTIONS: Read each story, then read each question. Read all the answers then mark the space for the answer you think is right. Mark NH (not here) if the answer can't be figured out from the story.

Earth is a large round planet. As it travels around the Sun it rotates, or spins. Let's say it is noon, and the Sun is straight above your head. Earth rotates, turning you away from the Sun. As Earth turns toward the east, the Sun seems to sink lower in the sky. When you can no longer see the Sun, your part of Earth is facing space, and the sky is dark. It is night. Earth keeps rotating until the Sun can be seen in the eastern sky. Before long, the Sun is directly overhead again. This is called a rotation. It takes Earth one day or 24 hours to rotate once.

Sun's light → daylight — Earth — dark

1. What is a good title for this story?
○ The Earth
○ The Sun
● Day and Night
○ NH

2. How many hours are in one day?
○ 12
○ 18
● 24
○ NH

3. What is another word for "rotate"?
○ Earth
● spin
○ eastern
○ NH

4. What causes Earth to become dark?
○ Earth turns west
● Earth turns away from the Sun
○ the Sun goes out
○ NH

5. What is it called when Earth goes all the way around the Sun?
● rotation
○ space
○ Earth
○ NH

6. When you can't see the Sun, what is Earth facing?
○ other suns
○ night
● space
○ NH

7. How long does it take for Earth to rotate once?
○ one week
● 24 hours
○ 2 days
○ NH

© Carson-Dellosa CD-3735   77

Name _____

Skill: Expository Passages

DIRECTIONS: Read each story then read each question. Read all the answers then mark the space for the answer you think is right. Mark NH (not here) if the answer can't be figured out from the story.

The earth has a north pole and a south pole. A pretend line called the axis goes from the north pole through the earth to the south pole. The axis is tilted, or slanted a little to one side. As the earth revolves, or goes around the sun, at times the north pole is turned toward the sun. When this happens, the northern half of the earth gets more sun and warms up. We call this "summer". At the same time, the southern half gets less sun and has "winter". When the earth goes to the other side of the sun, the southern half of the earth gets more sunlight. It has summer while the north has winter. The movement around the sun and the tilted axis are what give the earth its four seasons!

axis — sun — summer / winter — axis

1. What is the name of the imaginary line that runs through the earth?
○ north pole
○ south pole
● axis
○ NH

2. Why does each pole get more or less sun at different times of the year?
○ the earth spins around the sun
● the axis is tilted
○ the sun pulls away from the earth
○ NH

3. What is summer?
○ when the north pole gets sun
● when half the earth gets more sun than the other half
○ when the south pole gets sun
○ NH

4. What causes the earth's seasons?
○ north pole and south pole
○ the sun and the moon
● tilted axis and revolution
○ NH

5. How many seasons are in a year?
○ two
○ three
● four
○ NH

6. How long is one revolution around the sun?
○ one day
○ one week
○ one month
● NH

©Kelley Wingate CD 3735   78

Name _____

Skill: Expository Passages

DIRECTIONS: Read each story, then read each question. Read all the answers then mark the space for the answer you think is right. Mark NH (not here) if the answer can't be figured out from the story.

Summer is the warm season or time of year. Our part of Earth is tilted toward the Sun. It gets more hours of sunlight which helps warm the land, air, and water. During the summer, people wear light clothing and go swimming to keep cool. They wear hats, lotion, and sunglasses to protect their skin and eyes from the bright light. It is easy to get sunburned if you don't protect your skin! There are more hours of daylight than hours of darkness, so we can stay up later and enjoy the outdoors more.

1. What would be a good title for this story?
○ Keeping Cool
● Summer
○ Wear a Hat!
○ NH

2. What is one way to protect your eyes from the bright sunlight?
○ go swimming
● wear a hat with a big brim
○ put lotion on
○ NH

3. Which is true of the summer?
○ there are more hours of darkness
● there are more hours of sunlight
○ there are less hours of sunlight
○ NH

4. What do most people do during the summer?
○ eat more
○ drive to the mountains
○ stay inside
● NH

5. What wouldn't you do to keep yourself cooler in the summer?
○ wear lighter clothes
● wear a coat to keep the sunlight off
○ go swimming
○ NH

6. What does the word "season" mean?
● time of year
○ summer
○ protection
○ NH

7. How late do most people stay up during the summer season?
○ 10 o'clock
○ 11 o'clock
○ 12 o'clock
● NH

8. Why do we get sunburned so easily in the summer?
● the Earth is tilted toward the Sun
○ the air is so warm
○ Earth is tilted away from the Sun
○ NH

© Carson-Dellosa CD-3735   79

Name _____

Skill: Expository Passages

DIRECTIONS: Read each story then read each question. Read all the answers then mark the space for the answer you think is right. Mark NH (not here) if the answer can't be figured out from the story.

After it rains, the grass is wet and puddles are on the sidewalk. The warm sun and the wind work together to evaporate the water. Evaporate means to turn water into a gas called water vapor. The water vapor rises and sticks to small pieces of dust in the air. As the air rises it gets cooler and the water vapor condenses, or turns back to water. Dust and condensation gather in a group and form a cloud. As the cloud gathers more condensation, it gets darker. Soon the cloud cannot hold all the water. It falls back to the earth as precipitation. Precipitation is any form of water that falls from a cloud to the earth. The process of evaporation, condensation, and precipitation is call the water cycle.

1. What is the main idea of this story?
○ Precipitation is Water
● The Water Cycle
○ Clouds
○ NH

2. What does rising water vapor condensate on?
○ clouds
● pieces of dust
○ warm air
○ NH

3. What does the word "evaporate" mean?
○ disappear
● turn into water vapor
○ turn back into water
○ NH

4. How long does it take for water to condensate?
○ after a storm
○ until a cloud forms
○ three hours of sunlight and wind
● NH

5. Which of these things is not a kind of precipitation?
● dust particles
○ sleet
○ snow
○ NH

6. What is it called when water falls, evaporates, forms into clouds, and falls again?
○ condensation
● water cycle
○ precipitation
○ NH

7. How does the dust get into the air?
○ from farms
○ the water cycle leaves it behind
○ dirt blows into the sky
● NH

©Kelley Wingate CD 3735   80

Answer Key

Name _____

Skill: Expository Passages

DIRECTIONS: Read each story then read each question. Read all the answers then mark the space for the answer you think is right. Mark NH (not here) if the answer can't be figured out from the story.

One of the four seasons is the fall, or autumn. Hours of daylight and dark are about the same during the fall. The weather becomes cooler and living things get ready for the cold winter months ahead.

The foods we get from many plants are ready to be picked. Many of the summer plants turn brown and die. Their growing season is over. Other plants, like some trees, put their energy into their roots, letting the leaves slowly turn color and fall from the branches.

Animals gather and store nuts and seeds to eat later in the winter. They build nests inside trees or under the ground where they are more protected from the cold. Some animals grow more fur to help keep them warm. Many birds fly south, or migrate, for the winter.

People also use the fall to prepare for winter. Farmers gather their crops and store them in cool, dry places. People make sure their homes are tight so the cold winds won't get in. They take out heavier clothes like coats and sweaters to protect them from the cooler temperatures.

1. What is the main idea of this story?
- ○ Fall is a fun season.
- ○ Animals prepare for winter.
- ● Living things prepare for winter.
- ○ NH

2. What season comes after autumn?
- ○ fall
- ○ summer
- ● winter
- ○ NH

3. How do plants prepare for winter?
- ○ grow new leaves
- ● put energy into their roots
- ○ grow hard outer shells
- ○ NH

4. What is one way animal's _don't_ prepare for winter?
- ○ build warmer homes
- ○ grow more fur
- ● raise, gather, and store their food
- ○ NH

5. What do animals of the ocean do to prepare for winter?
- ○ dig holes on the ocean floor
- ○ grow longer fur
- ○ come to the land
- ● NH

6. Which way to prepare for winter is _not_ mentioned in this story?
- ○ migration
- ○ gathering food
- ● hibernation
- ○ NH

©Kelley Wingate CD 3735   81

Name _____

Skill: Expository Passages

DIRECTIONS: Read each story then read each question. Read all the answers then mark the space for the answer you think is right. Mark NH (not here) if the answer can't be figured out from the story.

Autumn is the season when many leaves change color and fall off the branches. Trees that lose their leaves are called deciduous. Do you know why this happens? A tree has many tubes, like veins, reaching from the roots to the leaves. Sap flows through the tubes, carrying water and minerals to the leaves. During the cold winter months, the sap would freeze if it stayed in the tubes. The tree would die with the sap all frozen.

When the weather starts to get cool, the sap goes down to the roots to stay for the winter. Without the water supply, the leaves slowly starve to death. They lose their green color and change to orange, yellow, brown or red. They can no longer hold on to the tree, so they fall to the ground. Maybe that is why so many people call the autumn "fall"!

1. What is the main idea of this story?
- ○ Why leaves are green
- ● How trees lose their leaves
- ○ Autumn is a nice season
- ○ NH

2. Where does the sap go for the winter?
- ○ it migrates south with the birds
- ○ to the leaves
- ● to the roots
- ○ NH

3. What causes the leaves to die?
- ○ they need food
- ● they need water and minerals
- ○ they need sunshine
- ○ NH

4. How long is it before the sap returns to the leaves?
- ○ six hours
- ○ twenty-five days
- ○ seven months
- ● NH

5. Why does sap stay in the roots all winter?
- ○ to kill the leaves
- ● to keep from freezing
- ○ to feed the roots
- ○ NH

6. What does the word "deciduous" mean?
- ● a tree that loses its leaves
- ○ sap that stays in the roots
- ○ autumn
- ○ NH

7. Why might people call autumn "fall"?
- ○ many people fall in the autumn
- ● many leaves fall in the autumn
- ○ it just feels like everything is falling
- ○ NH

©Kelley Wingate CD 3735   82

Name _____

Skill: Expository Passages

DIRECTIONS: Read each story then read each question. Read all the answers then mark the space for the answer you think is right. Mark NH (not here) if the answer can't be figured out from the story.

Winter is the coldest season of the year. Your part of the earth gets less sunlight and more darkness. The earth does not have enough sunlight to keep it warm. Many times the precipitation from clouds will freeze and fall as snow. Snow may cover the ground for a few months during the winter!

Plants stop growing and some die during the winter. Other plants and seeds are covered by the snow and must wait for spring to warm them up and make them grow.

Animals have a hard time finding food. Many will eat what they stored in the fall. Other animals curl up in a hole or cave and hibernate, or go to sleep for the entire winter! Some birds and insects may migrate to warmer parts of the world.

People do not have to hibernate or migrate. They wear warmer clothes and heat their homes to stay warm. Even the deep snows of winter do not stop people. They ski or ride snow mobiles that race across the top of the snow. Some people even invented a sport called hockey just for the winter.

1. What is the main idea of this story?
- ○ What animals do in winter
- ● The winter season
- ○ Plants and animals
- ○ NH

2. What causes the cold weather of winter?
- ○ snow
- ● sunlight doesn't warm the earth
- ○ the north wind blows
- ○ NH

3. What makes winter so hard for most animals?
- ○ there isn't enough water
- ● they can't find enough food
- ○ they sleep too much
- ○ NH

4. Which living thing is bothered the _least_ by winter?
- ● humans
- ○ plants
- ○ birds
- ○ NH

5. What sport was made to play in the winter?
- ○ baseball
- ○ soccer
- ● hockey
- ○ NH

6. What does the word "hibernate" mean?
- ○ to fly south for the winter
- ○ dress warmly and face the winter
- ● to sleep all winter
- ○ NH

©Kelley Wingate CD 3735   83

Name _____

Skill: Expository Passages

DIRECTIONS: Read each story then read each question. Read all the answers then mark the space for the answer you think is right. Mark NH (not here) if the answer can't be figured out from the story.

During the cold winter months, the sky is often full of gray clouds. The clouds are full of water, just like they are in the summer months. They become full of water and fall to the ground. However, the air between the clouds and the ground is colder at this time of year. The water drops that fall from the clouds freeze as they fall to the ground. These frozen droplets are called snow. Each snowflake is unusual because it freezes in a different pattern as it falls to the ground. The first snows of winter quickly melt when they land. That is because the ground is still a little warm from the summer months. As more snow falls, the ground freezes as well and the snow will not melt as quickly. The ground will freeze as far as three feet below the grass! The snow will melt and the ground will thaw as the weather gets warmer.

1. What do we call frozen flakes of water that fall in the winter?
- ○ rain
- ○ hail
- ● snow
- ○ NH

2. Why is each snowflake unusual?
- ○ they have seven points
- ● they freeze differently
- ○ they melt when they land
- ○ NH

3. What makes the water freeze as it falls?
- ○ it falls very fast
- ● it falls through colder air
- ○ it freezes before it falls
- ○ NH

4. Why is the air colder in winter than in summer?
- ● we do not get as much sunshine
- ○ Earth is farther from the Sun
- ○ it spreads from the South Pole
- ○ NH

5. How deep will the snow get on the ground?
- ○ three feet
- ○ two feet
- ○ five feet
- ● NH

6. What happens when spring comes?
- ● snow melts and the ground thaws
- ○ we get even more snow
- ○ snow freezes in new patterns
- ○ NH

7. Which sport would most likely not be done outside in the winter?
- ○ ice skating
- ● water skiing
- ○ snow skiing
- ○ NH

©Kelley Wingate CD 3735   84

Answer Key

Name _____

Skill: Expository Passages

DIRECTIONS: Read each story then read each question. Read all the answers then mark the space for the answer you think is right. Mark NH (not here) if the answer can't be figured out from the story.

Spring is the season that comes after winter and before summer. Our part of the Earth begins to turn back toward the sun. We get more hours of sunlight that help warm the air and ground. Snow melts and warmer rain falls. The grass turns green again. Sap returns to the trees, new leaves form, and plants begin to grow. Birds migrate north and other animals come out of hibernation, or a long winter nap. The earth seems to come alive with new growth. Many animals build new homes and have babies during the spring. This is the season where everything feels fresh and new. People put away their heavy winter clothes and take out umbrellas. Children put away ice skates and sleds. They take out roller skates and bicycles. Spring is here!

1. When does the spring season come?

  o **between summer and fall**
  ● **between winter and summer**
  o **between summer and winter**
  o **NH**

2. What changes happen to the Earth in spring?

  o **the ground and air get colder**
  ● **the sun warms the ground and air**
  o **rain freezes and the ground thaws**
  o **NH**

3. What are the first plants that grow in the spring?

  o **flowers**
  o **trees**
  o **grass**
  ● **NH**

4. What would be a good title for this story?

  o **The Animals Wake Up!**
  ● **Spring Brings Changes to the Earth**
  o **Put Away Your Sleds!**
  o **NH**

5. What does the word "hibernation" mean?

  o **building new homes**
  o **returning to the north**
  ● **sleeping all winter**
  o **NH**

6. What makes the Earth warm up in the spring?

  o **the wind blows from the south**
  ● **there are more hours of sunlight**
  o **it just happens that way**
  o **NH**

7. Why are animals more active in the spring than during the winter?

  o **they are too warm**
  o **they are not as tired**
  o **they are afraid of snow**
  ● **NH**

Name _____

Skill: Expository Passages

DIRECTIONS: Read each story, then read each question. Read all the answers then mark the space for the answer you think is right. Mark NH (not here) if the answer can't be figured out from the story.

Plants do not make babies the same way animals do. Plants make seeds that grow into new plants. Some plants make their seeds inside flowers. Roses, tulips, and daisies are some of the flowers that make seeds. Other plants make seeds inside their fruit. Blueberries, apples, and melons all hold the seeds of their plants. Nuts are also the seeds of plants. Pecans, acorns, almonds, and peanuts are all seeds. The pine tree makes its seeds in a cone.

Seeds get to the ground in many ways. Animals may eat fruit and carry the seeds to far off places. Squirrels gather nuts and bury them to eat later. Some of the nuts don't get eaten and may grow into new plants. Birds and bees help to spread the seeds of flowering plants. No matter how they get to the ground, most plants started out as seeds!

1. Which of these is not a seed?

  o **peanut**
  o **walnut**
  ● **apple**
  o **NH**

2. Which animals help spread the seeds of flowers?

  o **bears and rabbits**
  ● **bees and birds**
  o **squirrels and birds**
  o **NH**

3. Where does a cactus make its seeds?

  o **nuts**
  o **cones**
  o **leaves**
  ● **NH**

4. How do animals help make new plants?

  o **they plant seedlings**
  ● **they help spread seeds**
  o **they eat the flowers**
  o **NH**

5. Which of these plants makes seeds inside flowers?

  o **oak trees**
  o **apple trees**
  ● **dandelions**
  o **NH**

6. How many types of seeds are named in this story?

  o **two**
  ● **three**
  o **four**
  o **NH**

7. What would be a good name for this story?

  o **The Way Plants Grow**
  ● **Plants Come From Seeds**
  o **Seeds Taste Good**
  o **NH**

Name _____

Skill: Expository Passages

DIRECTIONS: Read each story, then read each question. Read all the answers then mark the space for the answer you think is right. Mark NH (not here) if the answer can't be figured out from the story.

Have you ever looked up into the sky and wondered about clouds? What are they? Where did they come from? Clouds are made when heat makes water evaporate, or become a gas called water vapor. The water vapor rises in the air until it starts to cool. It clings to small pieces of dust in the air and condenses, or turns back into a liquid. These small water droplets and dust gather together and soon form a cloud. Some clouds are thin wisps in the sky. Others are puffy and round, like balls of cotton. Sometimes the puffy ones turn gray or black. These clouds are full of water and cannot hold much more! Clouds help Earth, too. They give us shade on hot summer days. Clouds give us rain that makes things grow. Clouds also give us the snow that makes winter more fun!

1. What two things make a cloud?

  ● **dust and water**
  o **water and cotton**
  o **gas and water vapor**
  o **NH**

2. What is about to happen when a cloud turns gray or black?

  o **it will get warmer**
  o **it will get cooler**
  ● **it will rain or snow**
  o **NH**

3. How does heat help make a cloud?

  o **heat causes condensation**
  o **heat causes rain**
  ● **heat causes evaporation**
  o **NH**

4. What is another name for water that has turned into a gas?

  o **condensation**
  o **evaporation**
  ● **water vapor**
  o **NH**

5. In which way don't clouds help us?

  o **they give us rain**
  o **they give us snow**
  o **they give us shade**
  ● **NH**

6. What does "condensation" mean?

  o **turning into a gas**
  ● **turning back into a liquid**
  o **turning into water vapor**
  o **NH**

7. How big can a cloud get?

  o **as big as a country**
  o **as big as a mountain**
  o **as big as a continent**
  ● **NH**

Name _____

Skill: Expository Passages

DIRECTIONS: Read each story then read each question. Read all the answers then mark the space for the answer you think is right. Mark NH (not here) if the answer can't be figured out from the story.

Every living thing needs water to live. Is rain the only way water comes back to the Earth? Not quite. Water can fall from the clouds in a few different ways. During the summer months we usually get rain. Sometimes the air around the clouds is very cold, even in the summer, and the water freezes into balls before it falls. These ice balls are called hail. During the colder months the water passes through cold air and freezes as it falls. These frozen flakes of water are called snow. Sometimes the air is near freezing and the water falls as both snow and water together! This mixture of snow and water is called sleet. Any water that falls from clouds is called precipitation. Rain, hail, snow, and sleet are four forms of precipitation.

1. What is formed when water in clouds freezes and falls as ice balls?

  o **rain**
  ● **hail**
  o **sleet**
  o **NH**

2. What is this story about?

  o **snow**
  o **clouds**
  ● **precipitation**
  o **NH**

3. What do we call any water that falls from the clouds?

  o **rain**
  o **ice balls**
  ● **precipitation**
  o **NH**

4. What causes snow?

  o **the water freezes before it falls**
  ● **the water freezes as it falls**
  o **the water freezes after it falls**
  o **NH**

5. What affects the form of precipitation that will fall?

  ● **the air temperature**
  o **the size of the cloud**
  o **the temperature of the ground**
  o **NH**

6. What do we call it when rain, snow, hail, and sleet fall at the same time?

  o **crazy**
  o **snow-rain**
  o **sleet-hail**
  ● **NH**

7. What form of precipitation falls to the Earth as liquid water?

  o **snow**
  o **hail**
  ● **rain**
  o **NH**

Answer Key

Name _____
Skill: Directions

DIRECTIONS:
Read each passage then read the questions and answers. Decide which is the best answer to the question. Mark the space for the answer you have chosen. Mark the choice NH (not here) if the answer cannot be figured out from the information given.

How to Make Hot Oatmeal

1. Take out all the ingredients you will need: raw oatmeal; brown sugar; a saucepan; a spoon; a measuring cup; water; a bowl.
2. Measure one cup of water and pour it in the saucepan. Put the pan over high heat until it comes to a boil.
3. Measure 2/3 cup of raw oatmeal. Slowly add it to the boiling water, stirring as you pour.
4. Lower the heat and stir the oatmeal, making sure it is mixed totally with the water. Let it warm for six minutes, stirring every two minutes.
5. Remove the oatmeal from the stove. Spoon into a bowl and sprinkle with brown sugar.
6. Add a little milk if you like. Enjoy!

1. How many things do you need to make oatmeal?
   - ○ five
   - ● seven
   - ○ nine
   - ○ NH

2. Which of these do you do first?
   - ○ measure the oatmeal
   - ○ stir the oatmeal in the water
   - ● bring the water to a boil
   - ○ NH

3. How much oatmeal do you add to one cup of water?
   - ○ 1/3 cup
   - ○ one cup
   - ● 2/3 cup
   - ○ NH

4. What fruit tastes best on hot oatmeal?
   - ○ banana
   - ○ apple
   - ○ peach
   - ● NH

5. What ingredient do you sprinkle over the oatmeal?
   - ○ water
   - ● brown sugar
   - ○ cinnamon
   - ○ NH

6. How long should the oatmeal cook before you can eat it?
   - ○ 5 minutes
   - ● 6 minutes
   - ○ 10 minutes
   - ○ NH

©Kelley Wingate CD 3735   89

Name _____
Skill: Directions

DIRECTIONS:
Read each passage then read the questions and answers. Decide which is the best answer to the question. Mark the space for the answer you have chosen. Mark the choice NH (not here) if the answer cannot be figured out from the information given.

Get Ready for School

Before you can walk out the door, you must be ready to go! You can do this first group of things in any order.
- √ Get dressed (including shoes and socks) and wash your face.
- √ Eat a good breakfast. Be sure to have some fruit juice as well.
- √ Get your books and papers ready. Put them in a book bag or backpack to make them easier to carry.

The second group of things can be done in any order, but all of them must be done after the first group.
- √ Brush your teeth.
- √ Comb your hair.

This is the last group of things to do before you leave. They must be done in this order.
- √ Put on a jacket or coat if you need one.
- √ Open the door and leave.

1. Of these three things, which should you do last?
   - ○ get dressed
   - ● put on a coat
   - ○ comb your hair
   - ○ NH

2. Which of these should you do first?
   - ○ eat breakfast
   - ○ pack your books
   - ● get dressed
   - ○ NH

3. When should you pack your lunch?
   - ○ with the first group
   - ○ with the second group
   - ○ with the third group
   - ● NH

4. Which pair can be done in any order?
   - ○ get a coat and pack your books
   - ○ brush your teeth and get dressed
   - ● get dressed and eat breakfast
   - ○ NH

5. How many groups have things that can be done in any order?
   - ○ one
   - ● two
   - ○ three
   - ○ NH

6. In which group do you brush and comb?
   - ○ Group one
   - ● Group two
   - ○ Group three
   - ○ NH

©Kelley Wingate CD 3735   90

Name _____
Skill: Directions

DIRECTIONS:
Read each passage, then read the questions and answers. Decide which is the best answer to the question. Mark the space for the answer you have chosen. Mark the choice NH (not here) if the answer cannot be figured out from the information given.

Flying a Kite

1. Put together all the things you will need: a kite, a big ball of string, a strip of cloth, two sticks.
2. Put the kite together.
3. Poke or cut a small hole in the kite where the cross piece meets the long stick. Tie one end of your string to the sticks here. Make sure it is tied tightly!
4. Tie the strip of cloth to the bottom of the long stick. This makes a tail to help the kite fly.
5. Go outside and test which way the wind is blowing.
6. Hold the kite facing the wind. Run, let go of the kite, and let out some string!

Diagram labels: long stick, cross piece, tail, Back view of kite

1. How many things do you need to fly a kite?
   - ○ two
   - ○ three
   - ● five
   - ○ NH

2. Which of these do you do first?
   - ○ tie the string on the cross piece
   - ○ tie on the tail
   - ● put the kite together
   - ○ NH

3. What is the strip of cloth used for?
   - ○ to hold on to the kite
   - ● to make a tail
   - ○ to wipe your hands
   - ○ NH

4. What does the diagram show?
   - ○ front view
   - ● back view
   - ○ side view
   - ○ NH

5. What must be done as soon as you go outside?
   - ○ hold the kite facing the wind
   - ○ let go of the kite
   - ● test the wind's direction
   - ○ NH

6. Which item is not necessary for flying a kite?
   - ○ ball of string
   - ● heavy piece of wood or stick
   - ○ cloth
   - ○ NH

© Carson-Dellosa CD-3735   91

Name _____
Skill: Directions

DIRECTIONS:
Read each passage then read the questions and answers. Decide which is the best answer to the question. Mark the space for the answer you have chosen. Mark the choice NH (not here) if the answer cannot be figured out from the information given.

How to Make a P.B. and J.

1. Take out all the ingredients you will need: plate; butter knife; tablespoon; jar of peanut butter; jar of jelly; bread (any type).
2. Place two pieces of bread next to each other on the plate.
3. Open the peanut butter. Use the knife to scoop out some peanut butter. Spread it evenly on one slice of bread. Put the lid back on the jar.
4. Open the jelly. Scoop out one tablespoon of jelly and place it on the second piece of bread. Use the knife to spread it evenly on the bread.
5. Pick up the slice of bread with the peanut butter. Place it face down on top of the slice with jelly.
6. Use the knife to cut the sandwich in half.
   * This is even tastier with a glass of cold milk!

1. What do these directions help you to make?
   - ○ turkey sandwich
   - ○ jelly sandwich
   - ● peanut butter and jelly sandwich
   - ○ NH

2. Which of these do you do first?
   - ○ scoop out the jelly
   - ● put the bread on the plate
   - ○ spread the peanut butter
   - ○ NH

3. What do you use to scoop the peanut butter?
   - ○ a tablespoon
   - ● a knife
   - ○ a teaspoon
   - ○ NH

4. What happens after you put the bread together?
   - ○ eat the sandwich
   - ● cut the sandwich
   - ○ spread the jelly
   - ○ NH

5. How old do you have to be to make this kind of sandwich?
   - ○ six years old
   - ○ eight years old
   - ○ nine years old
   - ● NH

6. How many things do you get together before you begin?
   - ○ 4
   - ○ 5
   - ● 6
   - ○ NH

©Kelley Wingate CD 3735   92

Answer Key

DIRECTIONS:
Read each passage then read the questions and answers. Decide which is the best answer to the question. Mark the space for the answer you have chosen. Mark the choice NH (not here) if the answer cannot be figured out from the information given.

SWIMMING RULES
1. Pool opens at 8:30 a.m. (Monday through Saturday)
2. No diving at any time
3. Running near the pool is not allowed
4. No eating or drinking in or near the pool
5. A lifeguard must be on duty at all swimming times. If one is not available, you may not use the pool
6. Please shower before and after use of the pool
7. No pushing, pulling, or unnecessary splashing
8. No rafts, floats, or pool sticks allowed.
9. If you are warned about breaking any of these rules, the lifeguard may ask you to leave.
10. Pool closes at 7:00 p.m. (Monday through Saturday)

1. How many pool rules are listed on the chart?
- ● ten
- ○ twelve
- ○ twenty
- ○ NH

2. What time does the pool close?
- ○ 7:00 a.m.
- ○ 8:30 a.m.
- ● 7:00 p.m.
- ○ NH

3. What does rule number four tell you?
- ○ no running
- ● no eating
- ○ no splashing
- ○ NH

4. What should you do if a lifeguard is not on duty?
- ○ swim carefully
- ● stay out of the pool
- ○ use a float or raft
- ○ NH

5. When might the lifeguard ask you to leave?
- ● when you break a rule
- ○ if you don't have a swimcap
- ○ when he wants to have lunch
- ○ NH

6. What time does the pool open on special holidays?
- ○ 7:00 a.m.
- ○ 8:30 a.m.
- ○ noon
- ● NH

©Kelley Wingate CD 3735   93

DIRECTIONS:
Read each passage then read the questions and answers. Decide which is the best answer to the question. Mark the space for the answer you have chosen. Mark the choice NH (not here) if the answer cannot be figured out from the information given.

How to Make a Clay Elephant
Materials needed: cardboard; modeling clay; scissors; toothpick

Body: Roll a piece of clay into an egg shaped ball, use a piece of clay about the size of a ping-pong ball.
Head: Roll a piece of clay about the size of a marble into a round ball. Stick it to the body.
Legs: Make a clay "snake" about as wide as your thumb and twice as long as your hand. Cut the "snake" into four equal parts. Stick these legs on the body.
Trunk and tail: Make two smaller "snakes". One should be about the size of your little finger. Stick it on the head for the trunk. The other should be tiny. Stick it on the back of the body for the tail.
Ears: Make two small marbles of clay and flatten them. Stick them on the sides of the head to make ears.
Tusks: Cut two tusks from cardboard and push them into the clay on either side of the trunk.
Eyes: Use the toothpick to poke two little holes in the elephant's head for eyes.

1. How many materials do you need to make a clay elephant?
- ○ three
- ● four
- ○ five
- ○ NH

2. Which of these do you make first?
- ○ tail
- ○ ears
- ● head
- ○ NH

3. Which part of the elephant is made last?
- ○ ears
- ● eyes
- ○ tail
- ○ NH

4. How much clay should you use for the elephant's body?
- ○ the size of a marble
- ● the size of a ping-pong ball
- ○ the size of a tennis ball
- ○ NH

5. What part of the elephant is about as wide as your thumb?
- ○ trunk
- ○ tail
- ● legs
- ○ NH

6. How many elephants can you make from one box of clay?
- ○ 3
- ○ 10
- ○ 17
- ● NH

©Kelley Wingate CD 3735   94

DIRECTIONS:
Read each passage, then read the questions and answers. Decide which is the best answer to the question. Mark the space for the answer you have chosen. Mark the choice NH (not here) if the answer cannot be figured out from the information given.

Make String Art!
Cover your work area with newspaper and wear an old shirt!

Materials needed: 4 plastic bowls or cups, paper, 4 spoons, string, 4 colors of paint

1. Use a spoon to scoop some paint into a bowl. Use a different spoon and bowl for each color.
2. Cut four one-foot pieces of string. Hold one piece by the end and dip it into a color. Coat the string with paint. Use the other stings for the other colors.
3. Drop the paint covered string onto the piece of paper. Lift the string and drop it 2 or 3 time to make different patterns. Try wiggling the string to smear the paint.
4. Repeat step three using the other paint colors.
5. Set the painting aside to dry.
6. Use the paintings to decorate your room or make them into greeting cards.

1. How many bowls do you need to make string art?
- ● four
- ○ five
- ○ six
- ○ NH

2. Which of these do you do first?
- ○ cut the string
- ● cover the table with newspaper
- ○ spoon out the paint
- ○ NH

3. About how long should you cut the pieces of string?
- ○ eight inches
- ● twelve inches
- ○ sixteen inches
- ○ NH

4. Which colors of paint do you need to make string art?
- ○ red, blue, green, yellow
- ○ purple, pink, orange, blue
- ○ black, brown, green, yellow
- ● NH

5. How does the paint get from the bowl to the paper?
- ○ pour it out
- ○ use a paintbush
- ● dip string in paint and put on
- ○ NH

6. What is one suggested use for the finished art?
- ○ gift wrap
- ○ book covers
- ● cards
- ○ NH

© Carson-Dellosa CD-3735   95

DIRECTIONS:
Read each passage then read the questions and answers. Decide which is the best answer to the question. Mark the space for the answer you have chosen. Mark the choice NH (not here) if the answer cannot be figured out from the information given.

Easy to Make Gift Ideas

Soft Drink Can Banks: Rinse the can and let it dry. Use paint, felt, yarn, or paper to cover the outside of the can. Glue on buttons, ribbons, feathers or other trimmings. The can opening becomes the money slot.

Treasure Boxes: Use cloth, felt, or paper to cover a shoe box and its lid. Decorate the box by gluing on ornaments, patches, stamps, or whatever you like.

Pebble Pets: Choose ten or twelve pebbles or small rocks that have an unusual color or shape. Wash and dry them. Glue them together to create an animal, person or creature. Paint faces, fangs, scales, feathers, eyes, ears, or whatever you like on you "pets".

1. Which material is used in all three gift ideas?
- ○ paint
- ○ feathers
- ● glue
- ○ NH

2. On which gift should you paint a face?
- ○ Soft Drink Banks
- ○ Treasure Boxes
- ● Pebble Pets
- ○ NH

3. Which gift does not need to be washed before you make it?
- ○ Soft Drink Banks
- ● Treasure Boxes
- ○ Pebble Pets
- ○ NH

4. Which gift is made of metal?
- ● Soft Drink Banks
- ○ Treasure Boxes
- ○ Pebble Pets
- ○ NH

5. Which gift costs the most to make?
- ○ Soft Drink Banks
- ○ Treasure Boxes
- ○ Pebble Pets
- ● NH

6. Which gift is not used to hold something?
- ○ Soft Drink Banks
- ○ Treasure Boxes
- ● Pebble Pets
- ○ NH

©Kelley Wingate CD 3735   96

Answer Key

(Page 97)

Name _____ Skill: Directions

DIRECTIONS:
Read each passage then read the questions and answers. Decide which is the best answer to the question. Mark the space for the answer you have chosen. Mark the choice NH (not here) if the answer cannot be figured out from the information given.

Grow a Tree

Growing your own apple tree from a seed is not very hard. It just takes a lot of time to grow! **First:** Eat an apple. Be careful to save six or eight of the seeds. **Second:** Rinse the seeds in cool water. **Third:** Wrap the seeds in a paper towel or napkin and put them in a safe place in the refrigerator for about three weeks. **Fourth:** Put the seeds in a cup or glass. Cover them with water. Leave them in a warm place to soak for three or four days. **Fifth:** Plant the seeds in a small pot of soil. Keep them well watered. **Sixth:** When the seedlings grow to be three inches tall, separate them. Give each seed its own pot. **Seventh:** When the apple plants outgrow the pot, plant them in a special place in your yard. **Last:** Be patient! It takes a long time to grow into a good sized tree.

1. What do you do to the seeds in step four?
- o plant them
- o rinse them
- ● soak them
- o NH

2. Which of these steps should be done first?
- o wrap the seeds in a napkin
- o chill them in the refrigerator
- ● eat an apple
- o NH

3. How many years does it take to grow a full sized apple tree?
- o six
- o twelve
- o twenty-five
- ● NH

4. In which step do you plant the seeds?
- o second
- ● fifth
- o last
- o NH

5. What do you do in the eighth step?
- o put it in a larger pot
- o plant the tree in the yard
- ● wait
- o NH

6. In which step do you separate the seedlings?
- o fifth
- ● sixth
- o seventh
- o NH

©Kelley Wingate CD 3735   97

(Page 98)

Name _____ Skill: Letters

DIRECTIONS:
Read each letter then read each question about the letter. Decide which is the best answer to the question. Mark the space for the answer you have chosen. Mark the choice NH (not here) if the answer cannot be figured out from the information given.

September 12

Hi Keshia,
    The most exciting thing happened to me today! Grandma took me to the mall to shop for some new clothes for school. She let me pick out the shoes and pants I wanted. I let her pick out some skirts and a dress, but I liked them so it was alright. Grandma took me to SuperDuper Cuts and I got a really cute new haircut. Grandma and I agree that it looks very nice on me. After that we went to the food court for lunch. A lady kept looking at me and I was getting a little worried so I told my grandma. The lady came over and said she was a casting director for television. She thinks I should try out for a part in a new movie they are going to film! I will tell you all about it in my next letter.
                    Yours Truly,
                    Serina

1. Which person wrote this letter?
- o Grandma
- ● Serina
- o Keshia
- o NH

2. Which phrase is the greeting of this letter?
- o September 12
- o Dear Keshia
- o Yours Truly
- ● NH

3. What clothes did Serina buy at the mall?
- o socks, skirts, a dress
- o shirts, sweaters, a dress
- ● pants, skirts, a dress
- o NH

4. Which word best tells how Serina felt when the lady was staring at her?
- o anxious
- o curious
- ● frightened
- o NH

5. Why was the lady looking at Serina?
- ● she wants to put Serina in a movie
- o she wants Serina to sing on T.V.
- o she thought she knew Serina
- o NH

6. Why did Serina look so nice on the day she went shopping?
- o she had on her new clothes
- o she put on special sunglasses
- ● she got her hair cut a new way
- o NH

©Kelley Wingate CD 3735   98

(Page 99)

Name _____ Skill: Letters

DIRECTIONS:
Read each letter, then read each question about the letter. Decide which is the best answer to the question. Mark the space for the answer you have chosen. Mark the choice NH (not here) if the answer cannot be figured out from the information given.

October 18, 1999

Dear Brandon,
    I am sorry you broke your arm and have to stay home for a week. This morning the teacher told the class all about your accident and said that we should write a letter to you. I broke my leg when I was eight. I fell off the slide at school and landed the wrong way on my leg. I know how you feel about having that cast on. It is heavy and it itches a lot where you can't scratch it. However, it can be kind of fun at times. You will probably get less homework because you can't write with your hand now, and that is really neat! Everybody here at school can hardly wait to write their name on your cast. Besides, all the girls are already thinking up ways to help you when you get back! Rest up, feel better, and we miss you.
                    Your pal,
                    Brian

1. Who has a broken arm?
- ● Brandon
- o Brian
- o the teacher
- o NH

2. Why did Brian write to Brandon?
- o they are friends
- ● he wanted Brandon to feel better
- o the teacher told the class to write
- o NH

3. What is not one of the neat things about having to wear a cast?
- o kids want to sign it
- ● it itches a lot
- o everyone wants to be helpful
- o NH

4. How did Brian break his leg?
- o in a car accident
- o jumping from the swings
- ● falling off the slide
- o NH

5. How did Brandon break his arm?
- o in a car accident
- o jumping from the swings
- o falling off the slide
- ● NH

6. How long will Brandon be home from school?
- o two days
- ● seven days
- o fourteen days
- o NH

© Carson-Dellosa CD-3735   99

(Page 100)

Name _____ Skill: Letters

DIRECTIONS:
Read each letter then read each question about the letter. Decide which is the best answer to the question. Mark the space for the answer you have chosen. Mark the choice NH (not here) if the answer cannot be figured out from the information given.

December 27

Dear Aunt Minka,
    I know you could not get home for the holidays this year, but we all thought about you a lot. Momma said her plum pudding is not nearly as good as yours is. Poppa and Vinny often kept looking at the piano and sighing. It just wasn't the same without you playing our favorite songs while we sang along. Baby Kristie learned to say your name and she was looking for you, too. Even the cat seemed to be a little sad because you weren't here. I want you to know that I missed you just as much as they did, but I wasn't so sad about it. I took out all the letters you sent to me this year, and I read each one of them. It made me feel closer to you when I was reading your words. We will see you soon.
                    Your loving niece,
                    Denise

1. Why was Denise's family a little sad this holiday?
- o Momma made bad pudding
- o Baby Kristie was not well
- ● Minka did not come home
- o NH

2. Who wanted Minka to play the piano for them?
- o Kristie and Denise
- o Momma and Poppa
- ● Vinny and Poppa
- o NH

3. Where is Aunt Minka?
- o traveling the world
- o visiting friends
- o with her daughter
- ● NH

4. How do you know that Aunt Minka is a favorite person in this family?
- o Momma missed her pudding
- ● even the cat missed her
- o Denise read her letters
- o NH

5. How did Denise make herself feel closer to Aunt Minka?
- ● she reread all of Minka's letters
- o she sat in Minka's favorite chair
- o she wrote a letter to Minka
- o NH

6. When will Aunt Minka come home?
- ● soon
- o next year
- o in two months
- o NH

©Kelley Wingate CD 3735   100

©Kelley Wingate CD 3735   129

Answer Key

Name _____   Skill: Letters

DIRECTIONS:
Read each letter then read each question about the letter. Decide which is the best answer to the question. Mark the space for the answer you have chosen. Mark the choice NH (not here) if the answer cannot be figured out from the information given.

February 14

Dear Grandpa,

Roses are red and violets are blue,
I can't think of anyone nicer than you.
I looked for a card, but nothing was right.
None of them said the things that I might.
I wanted to ask you in some special way,
Would you please be my valentine today?

Happy Valentine's Day!

Your Valentine,
Jessica

1. Who wrote this letter?
- ○ Grandpa
- ● Jessica
- ○ Jessica's friend
- ○ NH

2. What do the first two lines tell Grandpa?
- ○ happy Valentine's Day
- ○ Jessica didn't buy a card
- ● Grandpa is a nice person
- ○ NH

3. What is unusual about this letter?
- ○ Jessica wrote it
- ○ it is for Grandpa
- ● it is a poem
- ○ NH

4. Where does Grandpa live?
- ○ Valentine Lane
- ○ Valentine Street
- ○ Violet Avenue
- ● NH

5. Why didn't Jessica just buy a card for Grandpa?
- ● none of them said the right things
- ○ she couldn't find a pretty one
- ○ Jessica didn't have the money
- ○ NH

6. What does Jessica ask Grandpa to do?
- ○ come to her house
- ● be Jessica's valentine
- ○ come to a valentine party
- ○ NH

©Kelley Wingate CD 3735   101

Name _____   Skill: Letters

DIRECTIONS:
Read each letter then read each question about the letter. Decide which is the best answer to the question. Mark the space for the answer you have chosen. Mark the choice NH (not here) if the answer cannot be figured out from the information given.

March 21

Hello Graham,
    I moved into my new house today. It is bigger than our other house. I even have a room of my very own! Mom said I can have bunk beds to put in my room and I can paint it any color I want. Do you think I should paint it brown like your room or gray like my old room? I stayed outside while the movers put the furniture in the house. A boy name Jake from down the street came over and asked me to go bike riding. He loaned me his old bike because mine wasn't unpacked yet. Jake showed me around the neighborhood and I met a few more kids. I ate dinner at Jake's house. He's a pretty neat guy. Don't worry, though. You are still my very best friend!

Yours Truly,
Phillip

1. What just happened to Phillip's family?
- ○ they ate dinner
- ● they moved to a new house
- ○ they painted a room
- ○ NH

2. Why does Phillip like the new house so much?
- ● he has his own room
- ○ it has a pool
- ○ it is in a nice neighborhood
- ○ NH

3. What color is Graham's bedroom painted?
- ○ white
- ○ gray
- ● brown
- ○ NH

4. Who is Jake?
- ○ Phillip's best friend
- ● Phillip's new neighbor
- ○ Graham's new friend
- ○ NH

5. What color was the bike Jake loaned to Phillip?
- ○ white
- ○ gray
- ○ brown
- ● NH

6. What words from the letter tell you that Phillip misses Graham?
- ○ "I can have bunk beds"
- ○ "he's a pretty neat guy"
- ● "you are still my very best friend"
- ○ NH

©Kelley Wingate CD 3735   102

Name _____   Skill: Letters

DIRECTIONS:
Read each letter then read each question about the letter. Decide which is the best answer to the question. Mark the space for the answer you have chosen. Mark the choice NH (not here) if the answer cannot be figured out from the information given.

May 5

Dear Miss Whitney,
    It has been a long year, but it is almost over now! Before summer vacation comes, I would like to tell you how I feel about being in your class this year. Last fall when school started, I wanted to be in Mrs. Sharp's class. You gave us homework on the very first day of school and you haven't miss one day since! You made me work hard and you never would take a paper that wasn't done the right way. I'll never forget that report I had to write seven times before you would let me turn it in! I thought I was unlucky to have you for a teacher, but do you know what? I learned a lot from you. I also had a lot of fun and I like you more than any teacher I've ever had. Thank you for giving me the best year I've ever had!

Your student,
Ken

1. Which person will get this letter?
- ● Miss Whitney
- ○ Mrs. Sharp
- ○ Ken
- ○ NH

2. Who is Mrs. Sharp?
- ○ Ken's teacher this year
- ● the teacher Ken wanted
- ○ Ken wrote to
- ○ NH

3. What is the purpose of this letter?
- ○ to say "I will miss you"
- ○ to say "You were mean"
- ● to say "Thank you"
- ○ NH

4. Which word tells how Ken felt about getting this teacher last fall?
- ○ wealthy
- ● unlucky
- ○ pleasant
- ○ NH

5. Which word tells how Ken feels toward his teacher now?
- ○ frightened
- ○ nervous
- ● thankful
- ○ NH

6. What grade does Miss Whitney teach?
- ○ first grade
- ○ second grade
- ○ third grade
- ● NH

©Kelley Wingate CD 3735   103

Name _____   Skill: Letters

DIRECTIONS:
Read each letter then read each question about the letter. Decide which is the best answer to the question. Mark the space for the answer you have chosen. Mark the choice NH (not here) if the answer cannot be figured out from the information given.

August 6

Dear Emily,
    My parents wanted me to get to know the "Great Outdoors", so they took me camping this summer. We camped right out in the national forrest near a lake, not in a campground. We had to fill our buckets with water at a gas station then drive it back to camp. There was never enough to waste, so I learned how to use the same water at least three times before throwing it out! At night the only light we had was from the campfire, the stars, and the moon. It was really dark out there, but I must admit that it was awfully pretty, too. There were a few wild animals that came through our camp. I got one chipmunk to eat right out of my hand. I also saw raccoon, deer, opossum, a hawk, and a skunk (phew!!!). I am glad we went camping, but I am also glad to be home.

Yours Truly,
Meghan

1. Whose family went camping during their summer vacation?
- ○ Emily's
- ● Meghan's
- ○ Susan's
- ○ NH

2. How did the family get the water they needed?
- ○ from the river
- ○ from a lake
- ● from a gas station
- ○ NH

3. Why did it seem so dark at night?
- ○ there was no campfire
- ● there weren't house or street lights
- ○ father would not turn on lights
- ○ NH

4. What animal didn't Meghan see during her camping trip?
- ● rabbit
- ○ chipmunk
- ○ hawk
- ○ NH

5. Which words best describe Meghan's camping trip?
- ● nature and faraway
- ○ comfort and cozy
- ○ harbor and friendship
- ○ NH

6. Where will Emily's family take their vacation next year?
- ○ Disney World
- ○ in Colorado
- ○ at the beach
- ● NH

©Kelley Wingate CD 3735   104

Congratulations!

_____

receives this award for

_____

Signed _____ Date _____

Congratulations!

_____

receives this award for

_____

Signed _____ Date _____

Way to Go!

_____

has completed

_____

Signed _____ Date _____

© Carson-Dellosa

Star Student!!

 _____

receives this award for

_____

Signed _____ Date _____

© Carson-Dellosa

Congratulations

receives this award for

Signed

Date

Congratulations!

receives this award for

_____

Signed _____

Date _____

Star Student!

receives this award for

Signed _____

Date _____

armor

© CD-3735

blind

© CD-3735

command

© CD-3735

cuddle

© CD-3735

approach

© CD-3735

author

© CD-3735

asleep

© CD-3735

cousin

© CD-3735

alarm

© CD-3735

attention

© CD-3735

character

© CD-3735

continue

© CD-3735

actual

© CD-3735

assistant

© CD-3735

burst

© CD-3735

consider

© CD-3735

difficult © CD-3735	expert © CD-3735	future © CD-3735	greedy © CD-3735
dictionary © CD-3735	equal © CD-3735	force © CD-3735	grateful © CD-3735
describe © CD-3735	distance © CD-3735	flock © CD-3735	goal © CD-3735
customer © CD-3735	disappoint © CD-3735	feast © CD-3735	glitter © CD-3735

imaginary	level	nibble	partner
hint	least	modern	paragraph
harm	laundry	miserable	opposite
harbor	journey	limit	obey

© CD-3735

prepare	popular	pause	past
© CD-3735	© CD-3735	© CD-3735	© CD-3735
receive	rapid	rage	prevent
© CD-3735	© CD-3735	© CD-3735	© CD-3735
rescue	repeat	remain	refuse
© CD-3735	© CD-3735	© CD-3735	© CD-3735
section	scrub	roam	riddle
© CD-3735	© CD-3735	© CD-3735	© CD-3735

slim	splendid	suggestion	thirst
simple	speech	stubborn	telescope
shallow	soldier	straighten	task
shaggy	slippers	sprinkle	sweat

© CD-3735

tremble	unusual	weight	yank

treasure	unload	wade	worst
© CD-3735

traffic	trust	visitor	wobble
© CD-3735

timid	trickle	usual	whisker
© CD-3735